Alexander Garden

Anecdotes of the American Revolution

Illustrative of the talents and virtues of the heroes of the revolution, who acted the

most conspicuous parts therein. Vol. 3

Alexander Garden

Anecdotes of the American Revolution
Illustrative of the talents and virtues of the heroes of the revolution, who acted the most conspicuous parts therein. Vol. 3

ISBN/EAN: 9783337214289

Printed in Europe, USA, Canada, Australia, Japan

Cover: Foto ©ninafisch / pixelio.de

More available books at **www.hansebooks.com**

ANECDOTES

OF THE

AMERICAN REVOLUTION.

Illustrative of the Talents and Virtues

OF THE

HEROES OF THE REVOLUTION,

WHO ACTED THE

MOST CONSPICUOUS PARTS THEREIN.

By ALEXANDER GARDEN, of Lee's Legion.

VOL. III.

REPRINTED:
BROOKLYN, NEW YORK.
1865.

ANECDOTES

OF THE

AMERICAN REVOLUTION,

ILLUSTRATIVE of the TALENTS and VIRTUES

OF THE

HEROES AND PATRIOTS,

WHO ACTED

THE MOST CONSPICUOUS PARTS THEREIN

BY ALEXANDER GARDEN,
Of Lee's Legion.

SECOND SERIES.

For their commendation I am fed,
It is a banquet to me.— *Shakspeare.*

CHARLESTON:
PRINTED BY A. E. MILLER,
No. 4 Broad-Street.

1828.

[The dedication which follows was written sometime previously to the death of General PINCKNEY. As a brief expression of the Author's exalted opinion of his talents and virtues, he is anxious that it should be recorded, and has in consequence suffered it to keep the place originally intended for it.]

TO MAJOR-GENERAL THOMAS PINCKNEY.

PRESIDENT-GENERAL OF THE CINCINNATI.

CHARLESTON, October 12th, 1828.

HONOURED GENERAL,

The cheerfulness with which you complied with my request, in furnishing me with a correct and circumstantial account of the Siege of Savannah, even when suffering under the agony of severe bodily affliction, demands the warmest expression of my gratitude. If my good wishes could avail, the speedy re-establishment of your health, would restore you, a blessing to your friends—your family, and your country. That steadiness of principle, and cool intrepidity, that proved essentially serviceable in establishing the liberty and independence of your country, might in all probability, be again required to support and direct our energies, against the encroachments of principles of Government, which will prove equally destructive of our prosperity and happiness. Permit me to offer, as a testimony of my respect, and high veneration for your character, the Second Series of Revolutionary Anecdotes, now published, and to subscribe myself with the sincerest affection and gratitude,

Your friend and most obedient servant,

ALEXANDER GARDEN,

Of Lee's Legion.

TO THE

MEMBERS OF THE HONOURABLE

THE SENATE OF THE UNITED STATES,

AND OF

THE HOUSE OF REPRESENTATIVES,

WHO BY THEIR UNCEASING EXERTIONS, AND IRRESISTIBLE ELOQUENCE,

CAUSED AN ACT FOR THE RELIEF OF CERTAIN OFFICERS AND SOL-

DIERS OF THE ARMY OF THE REVOLUTION, TO BE APPROVED

BY CONGRESS, AND TO BECOME A LAW ON THE 15TH MAY,

1828,

THIS COLLECTION OF

REVOLUTIONARY ANECDOTES,

IS RESPECTFULLY

AND GRATEFULLY DEDICATED

BY THE AUTHOR.

CONTENTS.

CONTENTS.

INTRODUCTION.

--- ◆ ---

" The evil that men do, lives after them
The good is oft interred with their bones."– *Shakspeare.*

I SHOULD consider it an indelible reproach on my country, were the recollections of the valorous achievements of her Heroes, and the enthusiastic attachment of her patriotic sons to her honour and interests, to perish with them. My strenuous efforts have been, and shall be exerted to the end of my existence, to keep them alive by giving them publicity, and to recommend them to our youthful candidates for fame, as the fittest models for imitation. The mite of applause, that from personal feeling, I am inclined to offer, is indeed small, but it is tendered with such admiration, and flows with such warmth from my breast, that I trust it will not only meet with favour from the public, but commendation also.

REVOLUTIONARY ANECDOTES.

PETITION OF THE AMERICANS IN LONDON TO THE THRONE.

THE following document is extremely interesting and ought to be preserved. It affords strong evidence of the attachment of the natives of America from every part of the continent to their sovereign, and a confidence in his justice and magnanimity unbounded, though fatally incorrect. The petition, which is firm without servility, was, in Carolina, so much approved, that the signers of it were greeted on their return home with a merry peal of bells, and the loud acclamations of their countrymen.

It gives me great pleasure to state that the sixteen last named gentlemen were Carolinians, and, that with a single exception, they remained steady in their principles and active in the service of their country, throughout the whole of the Revolutionary war.

3

FROM THE BOSTON CHRONICLE.

Petition of the native Americans residing in London, to His Britannic Majesty, in 1774.

MESSRS. EDITORS:

Having recently been employed in searching for old records, I met with a manuscript copy of the following petition of a number of native Americans, who were then in London, to his Britannic Majesty, in the year 1774. If you think it sufficiently interesting to publish, you are at liberty to do it.— Among the number of signers is the late ARTHUR LEE, of Virginia, a gentleman whose life and character seem to be but little known at the present day, although he was one of the firmest patriots of the Revolution, and his services, though not conspicuous, yet were eminently beneficial to the cause he had espoused. I was much gratified to observe, that this gentleman was not forgotten, on a late public occasion, and should be more pleased if the present era of good feelings should lead to the bringing forward of those eminent patriots, whose virtues are buried in obscurity.

It will be remembered, that the bills there alluded to are the last of the series of those acts of the British Parliament which produced a crisis, and were the immediate cause of the war of the Revolution : ·

To the King's most Excellent Majesty:

The Petition of several natives of America, most humbly sheweth :

That your petitioners, being your Majesty's most faithful subjects, are obliged to implore your gracious interposition to protect them in the enjoyment of those privileges which are the right of all your people.

Your Majesty's petitioners have already seen, with unspeakable grief, their earnest prayers rejected, and heavy penalties inflicted, even on the innocent among their countrymen, to the subversion of every principle of justice, without their being heard. By this alarming procedure all property was rendered insecure; and they now see, in two bills (for altering the government of the Massachusetts Bay, and the impartial administration of justice there) the intended subversion of the two other grand objects of civil society and constitutional protection, to wit, *liberty* and *life*.

Your petitioners most humbly represent to your Majesty, that to destroy or assume their chartered rights, without a full and fair hearing, with legal proof of forfeiture, and the abrogating of their most valuable laws, which had duly received the solemn confirmation of your Majesty's royal predecessors, and were thence deemed unchangeable without the consent of the people, is such a proceeding as renders the enjoyment of every privilege they possess totally uncertain and precarious. That an exemption of the soldiery from being tried in the Massachusetts Bay for murder, or other felony committed upon your Majesty's subjects there, is such an encouragement to licentiousness and incentive to outrage, as must subject your Majesty's liege people to continued danger.

Your petitioners and their countrymen have been ever most zealously attached to your Majesty's person and family. It is therefore with inexpressible affliction that they see an attempt, in these proceedings against them, to change the principle of obedience to government, from the love of the subject towards their sovereign, founded on the opinion of his wisdom, justice and benevolence, into the dread of absolute power, and laws of extreme rigour, insupportable to a free people.

Should the bills above-mentioned receive your royal sanction, your Majesty's faithful subjects will be overwhelmed with grief and despair.

It is therefore our most earnest prayer that your Majesty will be graciously pleased to suspend your royal assent to the said bill.

And your petitioners, &c.

Stephen Sayre,   William H. Gibbs,
William Lee,   William Blake,
Arthur Lee,   Isaac Motte,
Edmund Jennings,   Henry Laurens,
Joshua Johnson,   Thomas Pinckney,
Daniel Bowley,   John F. Grimké,
Benjamin Franklin,   Jacob Read,
Thomas Busten,   Philip Neyle,
Edward Bancroft,   Edward Fenwicke,
Thomas Bromfield,   Edward Fenwicke, jun.
John Boylston,   John Peronneau,
John Ellis,   William Middleton,
John Williams,   William Middleton, jun.
John Alloyne,   Ralph Izard, jun.
Ralph Izard,   William Heyward.

MECKLENBURG (N. C.) DECLARATION OF INDEPENDENCE.

It is a compliment richly due to our sister State of North-Carolina, to mention an important fact, which, however redounding to her credit, is even at this period but little known to the citizens generally of the United States.

The town of Boston has been, with great propriety, styled "the Cradle of the Revolution." The opposition of its inhabitants to the encroachments of Great Britain first roused the Colonists to a just sense of the injuries meditated against their liberties, and fixed their resolution to repel force by force.— Yet it will forever redound to the honour of North-Carolina, that it was among her people that the bold idea of Independence was first conceived and proclaimed to the world. The tyrannical measures pursued by the officers of the Crown ; the iniquities practised by those of the courts of justice, produced a general spirit of discontent as early as the year 1768. But it was in Mecklenburg County that a zealous opposition to the pretensions of the mother country, and a determination to resist the aggressions of power was first decidedly manifested. The leading men held meetings to ascertain the sense of the people, and to confirm them in their opposition to the claim of Parliament to impose taxes, and regulate the internal policy of the Colony. The Post Commandant of the county was, on one occasion, directed to issue orders to each captain of the militia, to elect two delegates from his company, to meet in general committee at Charlotte, the better to adopt such measures as should seem best calculated to promote the common cause, of defending the right of the Colony, and of aiding their brethren in Massachusetts. The order was issued

and delegates elected, who met at Charlotte on the 19th of
May, 1775. On that day, the first intelligence of the commencement of hostilities at Lexington, was received by the
committee. Its effect was decisive. The universal cry was,
" Let us be independent—let us declare our independence, and
defend it with our lives and fortunes." Resolutions were immediately drawn up and adopted. Dr. Brevard, who framed
them, had the honor to report them also—they were to this
effect :—

" *Resolved*, That whoever directly or indirectly abets, or in
any way, form, or manner, countenances the invasion of our
rights, as attempted by the Parliament of Great Britain, is an
enemy to his country, to America, and to the Rights of Man.

Resolved, That we, the citizens of Mecklenburg County,
do hereby dissolve the political bonds which have connected
us with the Mother Country, and absolve ourselves from all
allegiance to the British Crown, abjuring all political connex-
ion with a nation that has wantonly trampled on our rights
and liberties, and inhumanly shed the blood of Americans at
Lexington.

Resolved, That we do hereby declare ourselves a free and
independent people, that we are of right and ought to be a
sovereign and self-governing people, under the power of God
and the General Congress, to the maintenance of which independence we solemnly pledge to each other our mutual co-
operation—our lives—our fortunes—and our sacred honours.

Resolved, That we do hereby ordain and adopt, as rules of
conduct, all and each of our former laws, and the Crown of
Great Britian cannot be considered, hereafter, as holding any
rights, privileges or immunities among us.

Resolved, That all officers, both civil and military, in this
county, be entitled to exercise the same powers and authorities
as heretofore—that every member of this delegation shall
henceforth be a civil officer, and exercise the powers of a
Justice of the Peace, issue process, hear and determine contro-
versies, according to law, preserve peace, union and harmony

in the county, and use every exertion to spread the love of liberty and of country, until a more general and better organized system of government be established.

Resolved, That a copy of these Resolutions be transmitted by express to the President of the Continental Congress, assembled at Philadelphia, to be laid before that body."

I think it scarcely possible to read these Resolutions, without perceiving how strong the similarity of sentiment expressed in the Declaration of Independence, introduced by Mr. JEFFERSON, at an after period into Congress. Even the expressions are, in many instances, literally the same, in so much as to give conviction, that the Mecklenburg Resolutions were constantly in view, when the Committee of Congress drew that momentous document, which we consider as the palladium of our lives and liberties.

This early manifestation of patriotic enthusiasm, never knew diminution; a steadiness of principle characterized the inhabitants of Mecklenburg county throughout the whole war. It was there that supplies were, with the greatest liberality, bestowed on the soldiers fighting the battles of their country—that the hospitals were best protected, and comforts afforded the sick. It was there that the enemy met with constant and decided opposition, and that they were so incessantly harrassed at every turn, and in every situation which they occupied, that Charlotte was emphatically styled by them—"*the Hornets' Nest.*"

Of the zeal of the inhabitants in the vicinity of Charlotte and Salisbury, in favour of the cause of their country, my friend, Dr. William Read, has recently given me a striking proof. After the battle of the Cowpens, great industry was used by Lord Cornwallis to retake the captured prisoners; he was unwearied in pursuit, and it was imagined with considerable prospect of success. Under these circumstances, General Green directed Dr. Read to repair, with all expedition, to the residence of General Lock, near Salisbury, and tell him, verbally, that immediate exertion was necessary, and that he must raise, by the next day, one thousand men, to cover the retreat of Major Hyrne, to whose charge the prisoners were committed. Arrived at his house, Dr. Read asked if the General was visible, "he is at plough in his field," was the reply. "In what direction," said the Doctor. "This path," said a bystander, "will carry you to him." But a short distance was passed over, when Dr. Read met an old man on a sorry tacky, with a plough before him, to whom he said, "tell me, friend, where I can find General Lock."—"Come with me," was the reply, "and I will carry you to him." The route was now retrograde, and led toward the house: when the Doctor arrived there, believing that he was trifled with, he said in anger, "but where is the General?" "You shall see him immediately," was the answer. The old man then retired into a chamber, but returned instantaneously in a full suit of regimentals and large cocked hat, exclaiming, "*I am General Lock—your business with me friend.*" Dr. Read immediately delivered his message, when the old man replied, "it shall be done!" and immediately sending off his servants with orders to his officers to summon their men for duty, actually joined Hyrne the next morning (who had five hundred men of the 71st British regiment in charge) with a corps of one thousand mounted riflemen.

Nor were the ladies of Mecklenburg, in any degree, inferior in enthusiasm to the male population. I find in the *South Carolina and American General Gazette,* from the 2d to the 9th of February, the following paragraph :—

"The young ladies, of the best families, in Mecklenburg County, North-Carolina, have entered into a voluntary association that they will not receive the addresses of any young gentlemen of that place, except the brave volunteers who served in the expedition to South-Carolina, and assisted in subduing the Scovalite insurgents. The ladies being of opinion that such persons as stay lazily basking at home, when the important calls of the country demand their military service abroad, must certainly be destitute of that nobleness of sentiment, that brave, manly spirit, which would qualify them to be the defenders and guardians of the fair sex.

The Ladies of the adjacent County of Rowan, have desired the plan of a similar association, to be drawn up and prepared for signatures."

EMBASSY OF LIEUT. COL. LAURENS TO FRANCE, IN 1781.

I do not think that I can follow up the interesting document immediately preceding, in a more appropriate manner, or afford a higher treat to my readers, than by giving a particular account of the spirited conduct of Lieut. Colonel Laurens, when sent by Congress as a Special Minister to France, in the year 1781. Of its authenticity there can be no doubt. It was received by me in 1822, from my friend Major Wm. Jackson, of Philadelphia, who had been appointed at the request of the Lieutenant Colonel, Secretary of the Mission. It is due to Maj. Jackson, to give the statement in his own interesting and appropriate language.

" In the sixth year of the war of Independence, the events of the campaign had been very adverse to the American arms, and at the close of 1780, the resources of the United States were in extreme depression. General Lincoln, who commanded in the Southern Department, after a brave and protracted defence of Charleston, against the army and fleet under Sir Henry Clinton and Admiral Arbuthnot, was compelled to capitulate, and to surrender his gallant garrison, prisoners of war. By this success, and the subsequent defeat of General Gates at Camden, the British forces gained a control in the South, which threatened the most extensive and disastrous consequences. The main army, under General Washington, reduced by detachments to the Southern States, was badly clothed, irregularly provisioned, and without pay—the magazines were empty, the treasury exhausted, and the public credit of no avail. In this alarming crisis of the national affairs, General Washington convened a council of his most confidential officers—a faithful and minute representation was submitted to Congress; and, it was respectfully suggested, as the most immediate means of relief, that a Special Minister should be sent to France, to solicit a loan of money, and supplies of clothing and military stores, with a request that a naval superiority might rendezvous on the American coast at an appointed time, to enable the Commander-in-chief to undertake offensive operations against the dispersed posts of the enemy.

Congress acceded to the opinions of this interesting communication, and referred the nomination of the Minister to General Washington, whose selection of the "all-accomplished Laurens," justified the confidence of government, and secured the successful completion of this important trust. As Aid-de-camp to General Washington, Colonel Laurens was fully informed of every circumstance that could give furtherance to the negotiation; and, writing and speaking the French language with classical purity, he possessed, in an eminent degree, the power of illustrating all its objects. By the partiality of his gallant friend, the writer of this memoir was appointed Secretary of the Mission.

On the 9th of February, 1781, we sailed from Boston in the frigate Alliance, Captain Barry, and arrived at L'Orient in twenty days. Pursuing, without delay, his route to Paris, Colonel Laurens met the Mareschal de Castries, Minister of Marine, then on a visit to the Sea-Ports, at Hennebond, and having announced himself to the Mareschal, he very politely directed relays of horses to expedite our journey. On his arrival at Paris, Colonel Laurens entered on his mission with every advantage that distinction of character, ardent zeal of disposition, and consummate ability, to demonstrate the reciprocal interest of America and France in its successful accomplishment, could confer. Having delivered his credentials, and been graciously received at Court, memorials, explanatory of all the views and objects of his appointment, were presented to the Count de Vergennes, Minister of Foreign Relations, and they were repeated and enforced by personal intercourse from the 6th of March to the 2d of May, when Colonel Laurens conceived, from the protracted state of the negotiation, that it was the policy of the Cabinet of France, by delaying the aid which he solicited, to exhaust the power and resources of Britain and America, and to render both subservient to her views.

Under this impression, and a belief that this was rather the policy of the Ministers than of the King, Colonel Laurens decided to prepare a memorial, which should condense all the essential points that had been heretofore stated, and which he determined to place in the King's own hand. This memorial, embracing a luminous statement of facts, with clear deductions from them, was accordingly prepared—and, on the morning of the day, when it was to be presented, we went to the Cabinet of the Count de Vergennes, where we found Dr. Franklin and the Count.

Colonel Laurens, introducing the subject of his mission with his usual animation, was urging the necessity of a compliance with his solicitation, when the Count de Vergennes, in a manner at once smiling and sarcastic, observed—" Colonel Laurens, you are so recently from the Head Quarters of the American Army, that you forget you are no longer delivering the orders of the Commander-in-chief; but that you are addressing the Minister of a Monarch, who has every disposition to favour your country." Colonel Laurens, rising from his chair with some emotion, stepped to the opposite side of the room, and returning to the Count, expressed himself in nearly the following words—" Favour, Sir! the respect which I owe my country will not admit the term—say that the aid is mutual, and I cheerfully subscribe to the obligation—But, as the last argument I shall use with your Excellency; the sword which I now wear in defence of France as well as my own country, unless the succour I solicit is immediately accorded, I may be compelled, within a short time, to draw against France, as a British subject."

The force of this brief, but appropriate remonstrance, was keenly felt by the first diplomatist of Europe, and some time elapsed before the Count de Vergennes was sufficiently collected to say—" *Mais voila le bon Monsieur Franklin, qui est tres content de nous.*"—" No one," replied Colonel Laurens, " respects that venerable gentleman more than I do:—but, to repeat your Excellency's observation, I am so recently from the Head Quarters of the American army, that many circumstances of the highest interest are familiar to me that are yet unknown to that worthy man. I must now inform Your Excellency, that my next memorial will be presented to His Majesty, in person. I have the honour to salute you respectfully,"—and left the room. On reaching the door, Colonel Laurens asked my opinion of what had passed. I told him it exceeded all I had imagined of the interview. "No matter," said he "let us go to the inn and dress for Court, where the act must finish." [The Court was at this time in mourning for the Empress Queen, Maria Theresa, the Queen's mother—but we were indulged in wearing our uniform, with crapes on our arms and swords.]

"The Special Minister of the United States of America" was announced, and we entered the audience apartment, where the King was standing in the centre of a semi-circle, having the old Count Maurepas on his right, and the Count de Vergennes on his left.—Having bowed to His Majesty, Col. Laurens, instead of passing among the foreign ministers, advanced towards the King, and saluted him a second time, and, approaching nearer to him, presented the memorial, which was received under some embarrassment—for, although, as being an accredited Minister, it could not be refused, the innovation on the forms of the Court, was altogether unexpected, and the King passed the paper across the Count de Vergennes to the Marquis de Segur, the Minister of War, who put it in his pocket. The looks of all present marked their surprise. When the ceremonial of the Levee was over, we went to the inn, where we dined,—and on our return to Paris, in going by Dr. Franklin's house at Passy, I asked Colonel Laurens if he would not stop and see the Doctor—he said he would see no one until he knew the result of that day's proceeding.

The next morning, while at breakfast, he received the following note :—

"Mr. Necker presents his compliments to Colonel Laurens, and requests the honour of an interview at twelve o'clock,"—Here is something, said Colonel Laurens, let us dress and pay our respects to Madame Necker :—

On entering the drawing-room we found Mr. and Mrs. Necker, and the Late Madame de Stael, at that time a young lady about thirteen years old. The ladies having retired, Mr. Necker said to Colonel Laurens, " I have the honour to inform you, by instruction of His Majesty, that the loan which you solicit in your memorial of yesterday is accorded, the fifteen hundred thousand livres, which you request may be sent to Major Jackson, at Amsterdam, for the purchase of military stores, will be forwarded from Brussels—and any other accommodation, connected with my department, will be cheerfully granted."

On the next day a similar interview with Colonel Laurens was requested by the Mareschal de Castries, who said " I am directed by His Majesty, to inform you that the Count de Grasse, who is now at Brest with twenty-five ships of the line, bound to the West-Indies, will, conformably to the request in your memorial of yesterday, rendezvous on the American coast, at the time General Washington shall point out. The howitzers, which you want, cannot be furnished from the marine arsenal, as we have none of that calibre ; but Major Jackson will be able to procure them in Holland.—The frigate Resolue will carry you to America with such part of the money as you may wish to take with you—any other facility within my department will be accorded."

Thus was this important negotiation, which was certainly the hinge on which the success of the Revolution then turned brought to a happy close, by the wisdom and decision of a youth, who had not then attained his twenty-eighth year—but whose matured mind and heroic spirit, admitted no other rule of official conduct, than the honour and interest of his beloved country.

Having returned from the successful accomplishment of his important mission, in which he had negotiated the rendezvous and co-operation of the French fleet on the American coast, Col. Laurens resumed his military functions, and was eminently distinguished at the siege of Yorktown, where, leading to the assault of one of the British redoubts, he saved the life of the officer, who commanded it, and made him his prisoner.

Being appointed Commissioner for the capitulation on the part of General Washington, he met Col. Ross, of the British army, Aid-de-camp to Lord Cornwallis, and Commissioner on behalf of the garrison. Having placed the terms on which a capitulation would be granted before Colonel Ross, that gentleman observed—"*This is a harsh article.*"—Which article? said Colonel Laurens—

"The Troops shall march out with colours cased, and drums beating a British or a German march."

"Yes, Sir," replied Colonel L., with some *sang froid*, "it is a harsh article."

"Then, Col. Laurens, if that is your opinion, why is it here?"

"Your question, Col. Ross, compels an observation, which I would have suppressed.—You seem to forget, Sir, that I was a capitulant at Charleston—where Gen. Lincoln, after a brave defence of six weeks' open trenches, by a very inconsiderable garrison, against the British army and fleet, under Sir Henry Clinton and Admiral Arbuthnot, and when your lines of approach were within pistol-shot of our field works, was refused any other terms for his gallant garrison, than marching out with colours cased, and drums *not* beating a British or a German march." "But," rejoined Col. Ross, "my Lord Cornwallis did not command at Charleston." "There, Sir," said Col. Laurens, "you extort another declaration. It is not the individual that is here considered—it is the Nation. This remains an article or I cease to be a Commissioner."

The result was conformed to this just retribution. The British army marched out with colours cased, and drums beating a British or a German march. The march they chose was—"*The world turned up side down.*"

The war in the North being closed by the capture of this army, Colonel Laurens, impelled by ardent patriotism, hastened to the Southern army, where fresh laurels awaited his gallant exertions, and where his country was to witness his devotion, even to death, in her cause.

The writer of the present article, who was then Assistant

Secretary at War, received his last letter, in which he says—
"I am writing to you from a sick bed; but I have just heard
that Gen. Greene has ordered a detachment to intercept a
party of the British. I shall ask the command, and, if refused, I go as a volunteer."

Gen. Greene, anxious for the recovery of his health, would
have declined the request of Col. Laurens; but his determination to go as a volunteer, decided him to grant it.

It would appear, that by unavoidable accident, some troops
detached to the support of the party, did not reach Combahee
in time to prevent an attack by a very superior force—and in
the charge he was mortally wounded and fell from his horse;
his party cutting their way through the enemy.

Such was the close, while yet in its bloom, of his illustrious
life, through which he had exhibited such proofs of devoted
patriotism, heroic valour, and splendid talents, as would have
secured to him the first honours of his country, as they have
impressed the deepest regret for his loss, and the heartfelt
tribute of gratitude to his memory.

SIEGE OF SAVANNAH.

Furnished by an Officer engaged in the Attack.

Early in Sept. 1779, the Amazon French frigate appeared off Charleston bar: the Viscompte de Fontanges, Adjutant General to the army under Count D'Estaign, landed and conferred with Gen. Lincoln, when an attack upon the British force in Savannah, by the combined French army, said to consist of three thousand men, and one thousand American troops to be furnished by General Lincoln, was agreed upon.   By order of General Lincoln, Colonel Cambray of the Engineers, Captain Gadsden and myself, embarked on board the Amazon, then commanded by the celebrated circumnavigator La Perouse.   In a day or two after we left Charleston, we joined the French fleet, consisting of twenty ships of the line, and several frigates, when we went on board the Languedoc, to be under the immediate command of Count D'Estaign, who had desired that some American officers, acquainted with the French language, might be sent to him.   In passing before Beaufort, D'Estaign was apprised that Colonel Maitland, with a considerable part of the British force, was stationed at that place, and was aware of the advantages which would result from preventing his junction with the main body at Savannah.   Our progress was delayed some hours off the bar; and it was reported that some of the smaller vessels were preparing to enter, but the plan was relinquished because the pilots furnished from Charleston refused to undertake to carry them in.   This was the first great error of this short, but disastrous campaign.   The whole British regular force amounted only to two thousand five hundred men, of which Maitland commanded eight hundred at Beaufort; had these been prevented from joining Prevost at

3

*Major Pinckney.

Savannah, it is probable the latter would have capitulated, or certainly could not have made the same formidable resistance. I know, however, from the acknowledgement of the principal pilot, that he did refuse to carry in the vessels.

The fleet then proceeded off Savannah bar, where information being received that the British had a company of regulars posted on Tybee Island, D'Estaign determined to attack them. Accordingly, he landed with the officers of his staff, the three Americans, and his body-guard, composed of a Subaltern's command of about twenty marines; we marched near a half mile in the direction of the fort, when D'Estaign, looking back and seeing only his slender escort, asked the Adjutant General, where were the troops to reduce the British post? M. de Fontanges answered that he had received no directions to order any troops for the occasion. The General appeared much irritated, replying that he had informed him of the object he had in view, and that it was his duty to have brought with him the number of troops necessary for the occasion. While this was passing, a couple of Negroes came by, who being interrogated, informed that the post had been withdrawn early that morning. This extraordinary occurrence is mentioned to show something of the manner of proceeding of the commander-in-chief of the expedition, and of the footing on which he stood with the officers under his command.

The fleet then proceeded off Asseeba Sound, where about eighteen hundred troops were embarked in the boats of the fleet, and proceeded at night-fall twelve miles up the river to Beaulien. The order for landing, directed that the boats should follow, as expeditiously as they could, (in that in which the General embarked, a lantern was hoisted,) and on reaching the landing, the troops were to range themselves next to those whom they would find drawn up, without any regard to corps. It was fortunate for the General, whose boat being lighter than the rest considerably outrowed them, that a British post with two field pieces had been withdrawn the preceeding day, or the boats which arrived first, must have been greatly annoyed; the bluff of Beaulien commanding a long reach of the river up which they passed. The landing with such a body, would probably have been effected, but certainly not without considerable loss. No time was lost after the landing of the troops, in marching to Savannah; it appearing to be the desire of the General to arrive there before the day appointed for the rendezvous with General Lincoln.

The morning after the army encamped, within a short distance of Savannah, a Flag of Truce was sent in, requiring the surrender of the post and garrison, to the *Army of His Most Christian Majesty*. A delay of twenty-four hours for the answer, was required and granted; before their expiration, Maitland brought in his detachment, and the demand of capitulation was rejected.

General Lincoln, with the American army, arrived near Savannah at the time agreed upon, which was the 17th September, and on the 23d, the two armies formed a junction, and encamped together within about a mile and a half of the enemy's lines, the French on the right. Here I joined my Regiment, which being the first of South-Carolina, was encamped on the extreme left of the line.

It appeared now to be the determination of the Generals, to endeavour to carry the post by regular approaches; for the enemy's line of defence, which was scarcely begun when D'Estaign's summons was given, had, in that interval of ten days, become formidable; it extended along the sandy ridge or bluff, on which Savannah is built, from the swamp below the town to Yamacraw creek, which is its upper boundary. It consisted of a chain of redoubts with batteries, the whole covered in front by a strong abbatis. The principal battery appeared to be in the centre of the line, where stood, when we first approached it, a large public building of brick, but which disappeared in one night, and in a day or two a formidable battery was opened upon us from its site. The next work in importance was the Spring Hill redoubt, which was on their extreme right, and commanded Yamacraw creek, at the mouth whereof was stationed a British galley. This line was admirably adapted to the enemy's force; if it had been a closed line, their two thousand five hundred troops could not have manned the whole, especially as they were obliged to have some slight

works on each flank, and to pay some attention to their front
on the river, as the French had sent some small vessels of war
with a bomb-ketch into the back river, which is only separated
from the main channel by an island of marsh.   From the 23d
September,* when our army first broke ground, we continued
working in the trenches with great assidnity.   Our batteries
opened on the 5th of October, but though well served, appar-
ently with little effect.   The sap continued to be pushed forward until the 8th, when the remonstrance of the officers of
the French fleet against their being detained longer on the
coast, induced Count D'Estaign to inform General Lincoln that
he must withdraw his force; but to prove his desire to serve
the cause, he offered to co-operate in an assault upon the
British lines.   This appears to have been accepted as the *pis-
aller*, and on that day we were ordered to parade near the left
of the line at 1 o'clock of the next morning, where we were to
be joined by the French, and to march to the attack in the
following order:—The French troops were to be divided into
three columns, the Americans into two, the heads of which
were to be posted in a line, with proper intervals at the edge
of the wood adjoining the open space of five or six hundred
yards between it and the enemy's line, and at 4 o'clock in the
morning, a little before day-light, the whole was, on a signal
being given, to rush forward and attack the redoubts and batteries opposed to their front.   The American column of the
right, which adjoined the French, were to be preceded by
Pulaski, with his cavalry and the cavalry of South-Carolina,
and were to follow the French until they approach the edge of
the wood, when they were to break off and take their position.
This column was composed of the Light Infantry under Col.
Laurens, of the 2d Regiment of South-Carolina, and the 1st
Battalion of Charleston Militia.   The second American column
consisted of the 1st and 5th South-Carolina Regiments, commanded by Brigadier General M'Intosh of Georgia.   A corps
of French West-India troops, under the Viscompte de Noailles,
the Artillery, and some American Militia, formed the reserve
under General Lincoln.

* I kept no memorandum of the dates, but have referred to Gen. Moultrie's Memoirs for
them.

A faint attack by the South-Carolina Militia and Georgians, under Brigadier General Huger, was ordered to be made on the enemy's left; but, instead of the French troops being paraded so as to march off at 4 o'clock, it was near four before the head of that column reached our front. The whole army then marched towards the skirt of the wood in one long column, and as they approached, the open space were to break off into the different columns, as ordered for the attack. But, by the time the first French column had arrived at the open space, the day had fairly broke, when Count D'Estaign, without waiting until the other columns had arrived at their position, placed himself at the head of his first column, and rushed forward to the attack. But this body was so severely galled by the grape-shot from the batteries as they advanced, and by both grape-shot and musketry when they reached the abbatis, that, in spite of the effort of the officers, the column got into confusion and broke away to their left toward the wood in that direction; the second and the third French columns shared successively the same fate, having the additional discouragement of seeing as they marched to the attack, the repulse and loss of their comrades who had preceded them. Count Pulaski, who, with the Cavalry, preceded the right column of the Americans, proceeded gallantly until stopped by the abbatis, and before he could force through it, received his mortal wound. In the mean time, Colonel Laurens at the head of the Light Infantry, followed by the 2d South-Carolina Regiment, and 1st Battallion Charleston Militia, attacked the Spring Hill redoubt, got into the ditch and planted the Colours of the 2d Regiment on the berm, but the parapet was too high for them to scale it under so heavy a fire, and after much slaughter they were driven out of the ditch. When General Pulaski was about to be removed from the field, Colonel D. Horry, to whom the command of the Cavalry devolved, asked what were his directions. He answered, " follow my Lancers to whom I have given my order of attack." But the Lancers were so severely galled by the enemy's fire, that they also inclined off to the left, and were followed by all the Cavalry, breaking through the American column, who were attacking the Spring Hill redoubt. By this time the 2d American column headed by Gen. M'Intosh, to which I was attached, arrived at the foot of the Spring Hill redoubt, and such a scene of confusion as there appeared is not often equalled. Col. Laurens had been separated from that part of his command that had not entered the Spring Hill ditch by the Cavalry, who had borne it before them into the swamp to the left, and when we marched up, inquired *if we had seen them.* Count D'Estaign was wounded in the arm, and endeavouring to rally his men, a few of whom with a drummer he had collected. General M'Intosh did not speak French, but desired me to inform the Commander-in-chief that his column was fresh, and that he wished his directions, where, under present circumstances, he should make the attack. The Count ordered that we should move more to the left, and by no means to interfere with the troops he was endeavouring to rally ; in pursuing this direction we were thrown too much to the left, and before we could reach Spring Hill redoubt, we had to pass through Yamacraw Swamp, then wet and boggy, with the galley at the mouth annoying our left flank with grape-shot. While struggling through this morass, the firing slacked, and it was reported that the whole army had retired. I was sent by General M'Intosh to look out from the Spring Hill, where I found not an assailant standing. On reporting this to the General, he ordered a retreat, which was effected without much loss, notwithstanding the heavy fire of grape-shot with which we were followed.

The loss of both armies in killed and wounded amounted to 637 French and 457 Americans,* 1000.†—The Irish Brigade in the French service, and our 2d Regiment, particularly distinguished themselves and suffered most. The loss of the British amounted only to fifty-five.

Thus was this fine body of troops sacrificed by the imprudence of the French General, who, being of superior grade, commanded the whole. If the French troops had left their encampment in time for the different corps to have reached their positions, and the whole attacked together, the prospect

*Moultrie.   † Marshall.

of success would have been infinitely better, though, even then it would have been very doubtful on account of the strength of the enemy's line, which was well supplied by artillery. But if Count D'Estaign had reflected a moment, he must have known, that attacking with a single column before the rest of the army could have reached their position, was exposing the army to be beaten in detail. In fact the enemy, who were to be assailed at once on a considerable part of their front, finding themselves only attacked at one point, very deliberately concentrated their whole fire on the assailing column, and that was repeated as fast as the different corps were brought up to the attack. General Lincoln had the command of the reserve and covered the retreat ; if he had led the attack, I think the event could not have been so disastrous, and I am warranted in this opinion by the attack he made on the enemy's lines at Stono, where, when he found how strongly the enemy were entrenched, although his light infantry, on both flanks, had gained some advantage, withdrew the troops without any considerable loss.

The similarity in the result of this attack on Savannah, and that of the British on New Orleans in 1815, is remarkable ; the losses of the assailants and their enemies was nearly in equal proportion. Neither can Packenham escape the censure of precipitation, in urging the attack when he knew the scaling ladders he had ordered were not brought up, and before Colonel Tho'nton had got possession of our batteries on the west side of the river, which, if brought to bear on the right flank of the American line, must have made an important diversion in favour of his attack.

ASGILL.

Interesting particulars relative to the condemnation and subsequent enlargement of Captain Sir Charles Asgill, of the British Guards.

Sometime in the spring of 1782, a refugee officer named Lippincott, had caused Captain Huddy, of the American militia, (against whom it does not appear that any accusation was brought, or crime alleged, further than that of being found in arms, in opposition to the British troops,) to be executed without the formality of a trial, and, as it was generally believed, out of mere wantonness. Such a procedure, appeared to General Washington, so inconsistent with the laws of war, so great an outrage both of justice and humanity, as to determine him at once to resort to the fatal but necessary practice of *retaliation*. But, before any decided step was taken, a demand was made on the British Commander-in-Chief at New York, "That Lippincott should be delivered up to pay the forfeit of his crimes, and quiet the demands for vengeance, which were loudly called for from every quarter." No notice being taken of this demand, an order was sent, through Major Jackson, Deputy Secretary of War, to the commanding officer at Lancaster, where the British prisoners were confined, to select by lot, a *Captain* from among them, and send him under a guard, to the encampment of the main army, that by his death, he might atone for the murder of Captain Huddy, and convince the British Commander, who had evinced such extraordinary apathy, that every act of inhumanity exercised towards the soldiers of America, should be revenged by a similar act of severity. The lot fell upon Sir Charles Asgill, of the British Guards, and in conformity to orders, accompanied by Major Gordon, of the British forces, he left Lancaster for the head-quarters of the American army. In passing through Philadelphia, these gentlemen were received with great respect, and treated with every mark of attention by Major Jackson, who, to save them from the gaze of idle and prying curiosity, removed the centinel placed at the door of their apartment, and actually received them into his own quarters as his guests. The same delicate attention accompanied them throughout their journey. When he arrived at head-quarters, he was, by General Washington, committed to the charge of Colonel Dayton, of the Jersey line. To those who knew the mild and benevolent character of the American Commander-in-Chief, it is scarcely necessary to say, that to aggravate misfortune by unnecessary severity, was equally inconsistent with his principles and his practice. In his letter, dated January 11th, 1782, (several communications having been previously made) he writes to Colonel Dayton, " It is necessary that the security of your prisoner should be strictly attended to, but I wish at the same time, that all lenity should be shown him, consistent with his present situation." And again, in a letter to the same officer, dated June, 22d, 1782—" The only object that I had in view, in ordering the close confinement of your prisoner, was, that he might be perfectly secured ; but I am willing, and do wish every indulgence to be granted him, that is not inconsistent with that." That this conduct on the part of General Washington was sensibly felt, and properly appreciated *at the time*, appears evident from the following letter of Captain Asgill, himself.

To His Excellency General Washington, Commander-in-Chief of the American Army.

"Colonel Dayton's Quarters, Chat. May 17, 1782.

" On the 30th of the last month, I had the honour of addressing your Excellency in writing, stating the manner of my confinement, and the circumstances that induced me to claim your protection. Being ignorant of the fate of my letter, it would be satisfactory to me, if your Excellency would be pleased to inform me if it has been received. In consequence of your orders, Colonel Dayton was desirous of removing me to camp,

4

but being ill of a fever, I prevailed on him to let me remain
at his quarters, closely confined; which indulgence, I hope,
will not be disapproved of. I cannot conclude this letter,
without *expressing my gratitude to your Excellency, for ordering Colonel Dayton to favour me as much as my situation
would admit of*, and in justice to him, I must acknowledge the
*feeling and attentive manner in which those commands were
executed.*

" I have the honour to be, with the greatest respect, your
Excellency's most obedient servant,

CHARLES ASGILL.
"Captain First Regiment Foot Guards."

To what then, but the deadly animosity of a nation, instigated by the successful opposition to their arms, and the threatening prospect of the loss of empire, can be attributed the false-
hoods and scurrilities with which the British prints, on both
sides of the Atlantic overflowed. Their editors unblushingly
asserted " that Captain Asgill was *there* conducted to the foot
of the gallows, in order to complete the threatened retaliation;
and, moreover, that the instrument of punishment erected in
front of his prison, did not cease to offer to his eyes, the dreadful preparations, more awful than death itself."

The promulgation of these calumnies, could not fail to make
a deep impression where the truth was not known, and,
with a poignancy unspeakable, to lacerate and afflict the bosoms of his friends and family. I cannot, however, too highly
applaud the strong expression of maternal tenderness exhibited
by Lady Asgill, nor sufficiently admire the pathetic style in
which she endeavours to excite the generous sympathies of the
Count de Vergennes in favour of her son. No tale of woe
was ever told, that appeared more decidedly calculated to
excite interest, and move the heart to pity. The amiable
character of the victim, the heart-rending agony of his mother,
the delirium of his lovely sister, the sympathy of his friends,
caused every person, alive to the impulses of generous feeling,
to dread the catastrophe that so cruelly threatened the destruction of an innocent and unfortunate family. Still indignation

must follow the base attempt, to cover the character of General Washington with obloquy—and still more the effort, to attribute to foreign influence (a conclusion constantly insisted on) the safety of Asgill, which it is perfectly well known, proceeded from General Washington's calm and dispassionate examination of circumstances, and development of the fact, " that the murder, on the part of Lippincott, was not a wanton exercise of power, nor an act of cruelty proceeding from the pride of brief authority, but a deliberate act, sanctioned by *Governor Franklin*, presiding at a Board of *Loyalists*, and approved by *a majority of the members.*" The ground of complaint was thus completely changed. The demand for the person of Lippincott, who acted under the orders of a superior authority, was unhesitatingly given up. Of this Congress was immediately informed by General Washington, and their views of the subject according with his own, an order for the release of the prisoner instantaneously followed. They notice with *politeness* the zeal of the Count de Vergennes, in the cause of humanity, (and who would refuse to do so) but there is no hint given, no insinuation conveyed, *that to his letter Captain Asgill was indebted for his life.* A sense of strict propriety, caused the noble-minded Washington to alter his original opinions, and · ever averse to the indulgence of unnecessary severity, he gladly embraced the occasion of pleading the cause of an innocent man with Congress, and obtained their consent to set him free.

It should be remembered also, if further proof is deemed necessary to establish the anxious desire of General Washington to mitigate misfortune, and to soften the rigour of a separation from the friends that he loved, that permission was given to Captain Ludlow, of the British Guards, to *visit* his friend, and to Major Gordon to *remain* with him, by soothing attentions to beguile the tedious hours of confinement, and to give him fortitude to support the worst that might happen. The last letter of General Washington to Captain Asgill, speaks for itself—it needs no comment :—

"Head-Quarters, November 13th, 1782.

" Sir—It affords me singular satisfaction to have it in my power to transmit to you the inclosed copy of an act of Congress of the 7th instant, by which you are released from the disagreeable circumstances in which you have been so long. Supposing you would wish to go to New-York, as soon as possible, I also inclose a passport for that purpose. Your letter of the 18th October, came early to my hands; I beg you to believe that my not answering it sooner did not proceed from any inattention to you, or want of feeling for your situation. I daily expected a termination of your case, and I thought it better to await that, than feed you with hopes, that might in the end prove fruitless. You will attribute my detention of the enclosed letter, which has been in my hands a fortnight, to the same cause. I cannot take my leave of you, Sir, without assuring you, that in whatever light my agency in this affair may be viewed, I was never influenced, throughout the whole of it, by sanguinary motives, but by what I considered a sense of duty, which loudly called upon me to take measures, however disagreeable, to prevent a repetition of those enormities, which have been the subject of discussion; and that the important end is likely to be answered, without the effusion of the blood of an innocent person, is not a greater relief to you, than it is Sir, to

Your obedient servant,

GEORGE WASHINGTON."

Notwithstanding so satisfactory a termination of this eventful business, the British Gazettes continued lavishly to disseminate abuse, and even to assert, *"that Captain Asgill himself, was, on all occasions, loud in proclaiming the unnecessary rigour extended towards him by General Washington, and a scandalous want of delicacy on the part of the American officers, with whom he came in contact."* I was greatly surprised at these statements, and loath to believe them. I had been a school-fellow of Sir Charles Asgill, an inmate of the same boarding-house for several years, and a disposition more mild, gentle, and affectionate, I never met with. I considered him as possessed of that high sense of honour, which characterizes the youths of Westminster in a pre-eminent degree. Conversing sometime afterwards with *Mr. Henry Middleton*, of Suffolk, Great Britain, and inquiring, if it was possible that Sir Charles Asgill, could so far forget his obligations to a generous enemy, as to return his kindness with abuse. Mr. Middleton, who had been our cotemporary at school, and who had kept up a degree of intimacy with Sir Charles, denied the justice of the accusation, and declared, that the person charged with an act so base, not only spoke with gratitude of the conduct of General Washington, but was lavish in his commendations of Colonel Dayton, and of all the officers of the Continental army, whose duty had occasionally introduced them to his acquaintance. It may now be too late to remove unfavorable impressions on the other side of the Atlantic, (should my essay ever reach that far,) but it is still a pleasure to me, to do justice to the memory of our beloved Washington, and to free from the imputation of duplicity, and ingratitude, a gentleman, of whose merits I had ever entertained an opinion truly exalted.

Letter from Lady Asgill to the Count de Vergennes.

"SIR.—If the politeness of the French Court will permit a stranger to address it, it cannot be doubted but that she, who unites in herself, all the more delicate sensations, with which an individual can be penetrated, will be received favourably, by a nobleman, who reflects honour, not only on his nation, but on human nature. The object on which I implore your assistance, is too heart-rending to be dwelt upon. Most probably the public report of it has already reached you; this relieves me from the burden of so mournful a duty. My Son: my only Son, dear to me as he is brave, amiable as he is beloved, only nineteen years of age—a prisoner of war, in consequence of the capitulation of Yorktown, is at present confined in America, as an object of reprisal. Shall the innocent suffer the fate of the guilty? Figure to yourself, Sir, the situation of a family in these circumstances. Surrounded as I am with objects of distress, bowed down with fear and grief, words are

wanting to express what I feel, and to paint such a scene of
misery. My husband, given over by his physicians before the
arrival of this news, not in a situation to be informed of it.
My daughter, attacked by a fever, accompanied by delirium,
speaking of her *brother* in tones of distress, and without an
interval of reason, unless to listen to some circumstance which
may console her heart. Let your sensibility, Sir, paint to
you my profound, my inexpressible misery, and plead in my
favour. A word *from you*, like a voice from Heaven, would
liberate us from desolation—from the last degree of misfortune. I know how far General Washington reveres your
character. Tell him only, that you wish my son restored to
liberty, and he will restore him to his desponding family,—he
will restore him to happiness. The virtue of my son, will justify this act of clemency. His honour, Sir, led him to America;
he was born to abundance, to independence, and to the happiest
prospects. Permit me once more to entreat the interference of
your high influence, in favour of innocence, and the cause of
justice and humanity. Despatch, Sir, a letter from France, to
General Washington, and favour me with a copy of it, that it
may be transmitted from hence. I feel the whole weight of the
liberty taken in presenting this request; but I feel confident,
that whether granted or not, you will pity the distress, by
which it is suggested; your humanity will drop a tear upon
my fault, and blot it out forever. May that Heaven which I
implore, grant that you may never need the consolation, which
you have it in your power to bestow, on

                    THERESA ASGILL."

The news of the liberation of her Son, produced the testi-
monial of a mother's gratitude, in the letter which follows:—

" Exhausted by long suffering, overpowered by the excess of
unexpected happiness, confined to my bed by weakness and
languor, bent to the earth by what I have undergone, my sensibility alone could supply me with strength sufficient to address you. Condescend, Sir, to accept this feeble effort of my

gratitude. It has been laid at the feet of the Almighty, and, believe me, it has been presented with the same sincerity to you Sir, and to your illustrious Sovereigns. By *their* august and salutary intervention, as *by your own*, a Son is restored to me, to whom my life was attached. Yes, Sir, they will produce their effect before the dreadful and last tribunal, where I indulge the hope we shall both appear together, *you* to receive the recompense of your virtues, *myself* that of my sufferings. I will raise my voice before the imposing tribunals, I will call for those registers in which your humanity will be found recorded, I will pray that blessings may be showered on your head; upon him, who, availing himself of the noblest privilege received from God—a privilege, no other than divine—has changed misery into happiness—has withdrawn the sword from the innocent head, and restored the most worthy of sons to the most tender and affectionate of mothers. Condescend, Sir, to accept the just tribute of gratitude due to your virtuous sentiments. Preserve this tribute, and may it go down to posterity as a testimony of your sublime and exemplary beneficence to a stranger, whose nation was at war with your own, but whose tender affections had not been destroyed by war. May this tribute bear testimony of my gratitude, long after the hand that expresses it; the heart, which, at this moment, only vibrates with the vivacity of grateful sentiments, shall be reduced to dust, it shall bear out to offer you all the respect and all the gratitude with which it is penetrated.

"THERESA ASGILL.

" *To His Excellency the Count De Vergennnes.*"

The first of these letters, so replete with tenderness, so expressive of the anxious fears of an affectionate mother, gave birth to the communication which immediately follows. The second, so strongly indicative of her gratitude to the happy being who had endeavoured to succour and to save her, was the natural result of the interference to which she believed she owed the safety of her son.

Copy of a letter from the Count de Vergennes to General Washington, dated July 29th, 1752.

"SIR.—It is not in the quality of the Minister of a King, the friend and ally of the United States, (though with the knowledge of his Majesty) that I have now the honour to write to your Excellency. It is as a man of sensibility and a tender father, who feels all the force of paternal love, that I take the liberty to address to your Excellency my earnest solicitations in favour of a mother and family in tears. Her situation seems the more worthy of notice *on our part*, as it is to a nation at war with her own, that she has recourse for what she ought to receive from the impartial justice of her own Generals. I have the honour to inclose your Excellency the copy of a letter which Lady Asgill has just wrote to me. I am not known to her, nor was I acquainted with her son, who was the unhappy victim, destined by lot, to expiate the odious crime, that a formal denial of justice obliged you to revenge. Your Excellency will not read the letter without being extremely affected, it had that effect on the King and upon the Queen, to whom I communicated it. The goodness of their Majesty's hearts induced them to desire that the inquietudes of an unfortunate mother may be calmed, and her tenderness reassured. I feel Sir, that there are cases, where humanity itself exacts the most extreme rigour; perhaps the one in question may be of the number, but allowing reprisals to be just, it is not less hard on those who are the victims, and the character of your Excellency is too well known for me not to be persuaded that you desire to do nothing more than to be able to avoid the disagreeable necessity. There is one consideration, Sir, which, though it is not decisive, may have an influence on your resolution. Captain Asgill is, doubtless, your prisoner, but he is among those whom the arms of the King contributed to put into your hands at Yorktown. Although this circumstance does not operate as a safeguard, it however justifies the interest I permit myself to take in this affair. If it is in your power, Sir, to consider and have regard to it, you will do that which

will highly gratify their Majesties. The danger of young Asgill, the tears and despair of his mother affect them sensibly,
and they will see, with pleasure, the hope of consolation shine
on these unfortunate people. In seeking to deliver Mr. Asgill
from the fate which threatens him, I am far from engaging you
to seek another victim—the pardon to be perfectly satisfactory
must be entire. I do not imagine that it can be productive
of any bad consequences. If the British General has not been
able to punish the horrid crime you complain of, in so exemplary a way as he should, there is reason to think that he will
take the most efficacious measures to prevent its repetition. I
sincerely wish, Sir, that my intercession may meet success, the
sentiment which dictates it and which you have not ceased to
manifest on every occasion, assures me that you will not be in-
different to the prayers and to the tears of a family, which has
recourse to your clemency through me. It is rendering homage to your virtue, to implore it. I have the honour to be,
with the most perfect consideration, Sir, Your's, &c.

DE VERGENNES.

The order of Congress for the release of Captain Asgill, was
to this effect :—

IN CONGRESS—*November 7th,* 1783.

On the report of the Committee, to whom was referred a
letter of the 19th of August, from the Commander-in-chief, and
on motion of Mr. Williamson and Mr. Rutledge, relative
thereto,—and, also, another letter of the 25th October, from
the Commander-in-chief, with the copy of a letter from the
Count de Vergennes, dated the 29th July last, interceding for
Captain Asgill,

Resolved, That the Commander-in-chief be directed, and he
is hereby directed to set Captain Asgill at liberty.

CHARLES THOMPSON, *Secretary.*

Some further particulars relative to Captain Sir Charles Asgill, having come to my knowledge since making the above

statement, I think myself called upon by imperious duty to publish them, however decided their tendency to destroy the favourable sentiments I wished to inculcate of his candour, and veracity. The prepossessing traits of character that adorned his early years, I can never forget, nor is it possible for me to suppose, that to Mr. Middleton, whose entire family (with a single exception) were enthusiastically engaged in the service of America, he would have expressed a grateful sensibility for favour shown him, while in the circle of his more intimate associates, he had industriously propagated sentiments so decidedly contradictory. One circumstance, I confess, not only wounds my feelings, but staggers my faith.—That no reply was made to that highly interesting and pathetic letter of General Washington, informing him of his liberation from captivity, and freedom from the penalties that threatened his life, accompanied at the same time by passports, which enabled him to join his companions in New-York, and speedily to assuage the tumults of his mother's breast, and restore his sister to reason and to happiness, must appear strange, and in nowise consistently with propriety, to be accounted for. It manifested (to give it no harsher name) a want of politeness and respect, that with a *gentleman*, must be deemed inpardonable. If my opinions have been more favourable to him than they ought to have been, I sincerely lament it, since in the language of the poet I can truly say,

"I hate *Ingratitude* more than the sin of lying."

An American Gentleman, residing in London, wrote to Colonel Tilghman, formerly Aid-de-camp to General Washington, to this effect :—

" There are some persons here, who give credit to a charge exhibited against our good and great General Washington, by *young Asgill*, of ill-treatment and cruelty towards himself.—He alleges, that a gibbet was erected before his prison window, and often pointed to in an insulting manner, as good and proper for him to atone for Huddy's death, and many other insults, which *he believes were countenanced by General Wash-*

*ington, who was well-inclined to execute the sentence on him,
but was restrained by the French General Rochambeau."*

This letter was communicated to General Washington by
the father of Colonel Tilghman, (the Colonel himself being
dead before it reached America,) and was immediately replied
to by the General, in the following terms :—

"Mount Vernon, July 5th, 1786.

" That a calumny, such as mentioned by the correspondent
of your Son, has been reported, I knew. I had laid my account for the misrepresentations of anonymous scribblers,
but had never conceived before, that one, such as related,
could have originated with, or met the countenance of *Captain
Asgill*, whose situation often filled me with the keenest anguish. I felt for him on many accounts, and not the least
when viewing him as a man of honour and sentiment. I considered how unfortunate it was for him, that a wretch that
possessed neither, should be the means of causing in him a
single pang, or disagreeable sensation. My favourable opinion
of him, however, is forfeited, if being acquainted with these
reports, he did not immediately contradict them. That I could
have given countenance to the insults which he says were offered to his person, especially the grovelling one of erecting a
gibbet before his prison window, will, I expect, be scarcely believed, when I explicitly declare, that I have never heard of an
attempt to offer an insult, and that I had every reason to be
convinced, that he was treated by the officers around him, with
all the tenderness, and every civility, in their power. I would
feign ask Captain Asgill, how he could reconcile such belief,
(if his mind had been seriously impressed with it,) to the con-
tinual indulgence and procrastination he experienced ? He
will not, I presume, deny that he was admitted to his parole,
within ten or twelve miles of the British lines; if not to a *formal parole*, to a confidence yet more unlimited, by being permitted, for the benefit of his health, and the recreation of his
body, to ride, not only about the cantonment, but into the sur-

rounding country for several miles, with his friend and companion Maj. Gordon, constantly attending him. Would not this indulgence have pointed out to a military character the fountain from which it flowed? Did he conceive that discipline was so bad in the American army, as that any officer in it would have granted this liberty to a person confined by the express order of the Commander-in-chief, unless authorized to do so by the same authority? And to ascribe them to the interference of the Count Rochambeau, is as void of foundation as his other conjectures, for I do not recollect that a sentence ever passed betwixt the General and myself, upon the subject. I was not without suspicion, after the final liberation and return of Captain Asgill to New York, that his mind had been *improperly impressed ;* or, that he was *deficient in politeness.* The treatment he had met with, in my conception, *merited an acknowledgment.* None *however was offered,* and I never sought the cause. This concise account of the treatment of Captain Asgill, is given from a hasty recollection of the circumstances. If I had time, and it were essential, by unpacking my papers and recurring to authentic files, I might have been more pointed and full. It is in my power at any time to convince the *unbiassed mind,* that my conduct, throughout the whole of this business, was, neither influenced by passion, guided by inhumanity, or under the control of *any interference whatsoever.* I essayed every thing to save the innocent, bring the guilty to punishment, and stop the further perpetration of similar crimes. With what success the impartial world must, and certainly will decide. With very great esteem and regard, I have the honour to be, dear Sir, your most obedient servant,

GEORGE WASHINGTON."

" *To James Tilghman, Esq.*"

PATRIOTIC CONDUCT OF THE AMERICAN LADIES.

I HAVE been accused of lavishly bestowing encomiums on the patriotism of the Ladies of South-Carolina, while I scarcely noticed the meritorious conduct of females, equally distinguished, in other parts of the Union. However appearances may condemn me, I cannot attribute, to myself, the fault of intentional neglect; I gave details of occurrences, that I knew to be correct; but ventured not, on mere report, to speak of events abroad, that, however honourable to my country, might prove, on being particularly inquired into, false and exaggerated. With the increase of knowledge came also an ardent desire to bestow the palm of merit wheresoever it had been acquired; and I, as much delighted to celebrate the unremitted zeal of the ladies of Philadelphia, and of Trenton, raising funds for the succour and support of the army, wasted by disease, and perishing under the accumulated miseries of famine and nakedness, as in presenting to public view the patient sufferings and resistance to oppression, by the fair daughters of Carolina. I will say still more. Confident I am, that the intrepidity of the sainted being,* who afterwards honoured me with her hand, in rescuing from a position of extreme danger, her infant relative, Colonel Fenwick, did not in a higher degree excite my admiration and applause, than the bold and unshaken courage of the lady of whom I am now about to speak.

MRS. BORDEN.

At a period when the cloud of misfortune obscured the bright prospects of America, and even to our most sanguine patriots, the expectation of establishing our independence ap-

* Miss Mary Anna Gibbs.

peared but a visionary dream ; when New-York and Rhode-
Island were quietly possessed by the British armies, and the
Jerseys overrun by their victorious Generals, opposed but a
feeble resistance to their overwhelming power, a British officer,* of the highest rank, commanding a large division of their
troops, stationed at Bordentown, addressing Mrs. Borden, who
resided on her estate in a mansion of superior elegance, demanded in an authoritative tone, " Where, Madam, is your
rebel husband—where your rebel son ?" " Doing their duty
to their country, under the orders of Gen. Washington," was
the prompt reply. " We are well apprized" rejoined the officer, " of the influence you possess, over the political creed of
your family, and that to them your opinion is law. Be wise,
then, in time, and while mercy is tendered to you, fail not to
accept it. Bid them quit the standard of rebellion, and cordially unite with us, in bringing his Majesty's deluded subjects
to submission, and a proper sense of their errors and ingratitude, to the best of kings. Your property will then be protected, and remain without injury in your possession. But,
should you hesitate to profit by our clemency, the wasting of
your estate and destruction of your mansion will inevitably
follow." " Begin, then, the havock which you threaten," replied the heroic lady, " the sight of my house in flames, would
be to me a treat, for, I have seen enough of you to know, that
you never injure, what it is possible for you to keep and enjoy.
The application of a torch to it I should regard as a signal for
your departure, and consider the retreat of the spoiler an ample compensation for the loss of my property."

This was one of those threats, which the British never failed
to carry into execution. The house was burnt, and the whole
property consigned to waste and desolation. But, as had been
foreseen, the perpetrator of the ruthless deed, retreated to return no more.

* Lord Cornwallis.

LYDIA DARRAH.

THE anecdote which follows is fully detailed by the editor of the *American Quarterly Review*, in the first number of his interesting publication. It has been in my possession since the year 1822, when it was presented to me by that respectable gentleman himself. In some immaterial points our statements differ; yet, as the narrative affords a trait of heroism, creditable to the patriotic firmness of a female of our country, I am confident that I shall not offend him by giving it a place in my collections.

The superior officers of the British army, were accustomed to hold their consultations on all subjects of importance at the house of William and Lydia Darrah, members of the Society of Friends, immediately opposite to the quarters of the Commander-in-chief, in Second-street. It was in December, in the year that they occupied the city, that the Adjutant General of the army desired Lydia to have an apartment prepared for the reception of himself and friends, and to order her family early to bed: adding, when ready to depart, notice shall be given to you to let us out, and to extinguish the fire and candles. The manner of delivering this order, especially that part of it which commanded the early retirement of her family, strongly excited Lydia's curiosity, and determined her, if possible, to discover the mystery of their meeting. Approaching without shoes, the room in which the conference was held, and placing her ear to the key-hole, she heard the order read for the troops to quit the city on the night of the 4th, to attack the American army encamped at White Marsh. Returning immediately to her room, she laid herself down, but in a little while, a loud knocking at the door, which for some time she pretended not to hear, proclaimed the intention of the party to retire. Having let them out, she again sought her bed, but not to sleep; the agitation

of her mind precluded the possibility of enjoying it. She
thought only of the dangers that threatened the lives of thou-
sands of her countrymen, and believing it to be in her power
to avert the evil, determined at all hazards to apprize General
Washington of his danger. Telling her husband at early dawn,
that flour was wanting for domestic purposes, and that she
should go to Frankford to obtain it. She repaired to Head
Quarters, got access to General Howe, and obtained permission
to pass the British lines. Leaving her bag at the mill, Lydia
now pressed forward towards the American army, and meeting
Captain Allen M'Lean, an officer from his superior intelligence
and activity, selected by General Washington to gain intelligence, discovered to him the important secret, obtaining his
promise not to jeopardize her safety by telling from whom he
had obtained it. Captain M'Lean with all speed informed the
Commander-in-chief of his danger, who, of course, took every
necessary step to baffle the contemplated enterprize, and to
show the enemy that he was prepared to receive them. Lydia
returned home with her flour, secretly watched the movements
of the British army, and saw them depart. Her anxiety during their absence was excessive, nor was it lessened when on
their return the Adjutant General summoning her to his apartment and locking the door with an air of mystery, demanded
" Whether any of the family were up on the night that he had
received company at her house?" She told him, "that without
an exception, they had all retired at 8 o'clock." "You, I
know, Lydia, were asleep, for I knocked at your door three
times before you heard me, yet, although I am at a loss to conceive who gave the information of our intended attack to General Washington, it is certain that we were betrayed. For, on
arriving near his encampment, we found his cannon mounted
—his troops under arms, and at every point so perfectly prepared to receive us that we were compelled like fools to make
a retrograde movement, without inflicting on our enemy any
manner of injury whatsoever."

The editor of the *Quarterly Review*, designates Lt. Colonel
Craig, as the American officer to whom Lydia communicated

her important intelligence. Judge Marshall, in his Memoirs, appears to think as I do, that it was to Colonel M'Lean.

The anecdote which follows, being highly creditable to female patriotism, is recorded by me with peculiar delight :—

ESCAPE OF CAPTAIN PLUNKETT.

Captain Plunkett, a high-spirited Irishman, whose attachment to the cause of liberty had led him to seek a commission in the Continental army, had, by the chances of war, been compelled to give up his sword, and to surrender himself a prisoner to the enemy. Previously to this untoward event, by the suavity of his manners, and uniformly correct conduct, he had rendered himself an acceptable guest in many families in Philadelphia, and particularly so, to one of the Society of Friends, who, however averse to warfare, were not insensible of the claims of those to their regard, who, by the exercise of manly and generous feelings, delighted to soften its asperities. There was among them a female, mild and gentle as a dove, yet, in firmness of mind, a heroine, and in personal charms an angel. She saw the sufferings of the captive soldier, and under the influences of pity, or perhaps a more powerful passion, resolved, at all hazards to relieve him. It accidentally happened, that the uniform of Captain Plunkett's Regiment bore a striking resemblance to that of a British corps, which was frequently set as a guard over the prison in which he was confined. A new suit of regimentals was in consequence procured and conveyed, without suspicion of sinister design, to the Captain. On the judicious use of these rested the hopes of the fair Friend to give him freedom. It frequently happened that officers of inferior grade, while their superiors affected to shun all intercourse with rebels, would enter the apartments of the prisoners, and converse with them with kindness and familiarity, and then at their pleasure retire. Two centinels constantly walked the rounds without, and the practice of seeing their officers walking in and out of the interior prison, became so familiar,

6

as scarcely to attract notice, and constantly caused them to
give way without hesitation, as often as an officer showed a
disposition to retire. Captain Plunkett took the advantage of
this circumstance, and putting on his new coat, at the moment
that the relief of the Guard was taking place, sallied forth,
twirling a switch carelessly about and ordering the exterior
door of the prison to be opened, walked without opposition
into the street. Repairing without delay to the habitation of
his fair friend, he was received with kindness, and for some
days secreted and cherished with every manifestation of affectionate regard. To elude the vigilance of the British Guards,
if he attempted to pass into the country, in his present dress,
was deemed impossible. Woman's wit, however, is never at a
loss for contrivances, while swayed by the influences of love or
benevolence. Both, in this instance, may have aided invention. Plunkett had three strong claims in his favour: he was
a handsome man—a soldier—and an Irishman. The general
propensity of the Quakers, in favor of the Royal cause, ex-
empted the sect in a great measure from suspicion, in so great
a degree indeed, that the barriers of the city were generally
entrusted to the care of their members, as the best judges of
the characters of those persons who might be allowed to pass
them, without injury to the British interests. A female Friend,
of low origin, officiating as a servant in a farm near the city,
was in the family, on a visit to a relative. A pretext was
formed to present her with a new suit of clothes, in order to
possess that which she wore when she entered the city. Captain Plunkett was immediately disguised as a woman, and appeared at the barrier accompanied by his anxious deliverer.
" Friend Roberts," said the enterprising enthusiast, " may
this damsel and myself pass to visit a friend at a neighbouring
farm ?" " Certainly," said Roberts, " go forward." The city
was speedily left behind, and Capt. Plunkett found himself
safe under the protection of Colonel Allen M'Lean, his particular friend, from whose lips I received the anecdote now recorded.

PENNSYLVANIA LADIES.

BEFORE I enter into particulars relative to the exemplary conduct of the Ladies of Philadelphia, I would notice a publication in the Philadelphia papers, dated June, 1780, under the title

"THE SENTIMENTS OF AN AMERICAN WOMAN."

[FROM NILES' REGISTER.]

" On the commencement of actual war, the women of America manifested a firm resolution to contribute as much as could depend on them, to the deliverance of their country. Animated by the purest patriotism, they are sensible of sorrow at this day, in not offering more than barren wishes for the success of so glorious a revolution. They aspire to render themselves more really useful, and this sentiment is universal, from the North to the South of the thirteen United States. Our ambition is kindled by the fame of those heroines of antiquity, who have made their sex illustrious, and have proved to the universe, that of the weakness of our constitution, if opinions and manners did not forbid us to march to glory by the same paths as the men, we should at least equal and sometimes surpass them in our love for the public good. I glory in all that my sex has done great and commendable. I call to mind with enthusiasm, and with admiration, all those acts of courage, of constancy and patriotism, which history has transmitted to us. The people, favoured by Heaven, preserved from destruction by the virtue, the zeal, and the resolution of Deborah, of Judith, of Esther! The fortitude of the mother of the Maccabees, in giving up her sons to die before her eyes. Rome, saved from the fury of a victorious enemy by the efforts of Volumnia, and other Roman ladies. So many famous sieges, where the women have been seen forgetting the weakness of their sex, building new walls, digging trenches with their feeble hands, and furnishing arms to their defenders; they themselves darting the

missile weapons on the enemy—resigning the ornaments of
their apparel, and their fortunes to fill the public treasury, and
to hasten to deliver their country—burying themselves under
the ruins—throwing themselves into the flames, rather than
submit to the disgrace of humiliation, before a proud and
haughty enemy. Born for liberty, disdaining to bear the oppression of a tyrannic government, we associate ourselves to
the grandeur of those sovereigns, cherished and revered, who
have held with so much splendor the sceptre of the greatest
States. The Matildas, the Elizabeth's, the Mary's, and the
Catharine's, and have extended the empire of liberty, and contented to reign by sweetness and justice, have broken the chains
of slavery, forged by tyrants in the times of ignorance and barbarity. The Spanish women—do they not make at this moment, the most patriotic sacrifices, to increase the means of victory in the hands of their sovereign ? He is a friend to the
French nation. They are our allies. We call to mind, doubly
interested, that it was a French maid, who kindled up among her
fellow-citizens the flame of patriotism, buried under long mis-
fortunes. It was the Maid of Orleans, who drove from the
kingdom of France the ancestors of those same British, whose
odious yoke we have just shaken off, and whom it is necessary
that we should drive from the continent. But I will limit myself to this small number of achievements.—Who knows if persons disposed to censure, and sometimes too severely, with regard to us, may not disapprove our appearing acquainted even
with the actions of which our sex boast ? We are at least certain, that he cannot be a good citizen, who will not applaud our
effort for the relief of the armies, which defend our lives, our
possessions, our liberties. The situation of our soldiery has
been presented to me, the evils inseparable from war, and the
firm and generous spirit, which has enabled them to support
these. But, it has been said, that they may apprehend, that in
the course of a long war, the view of their distresses may be
lost, and their services forgotten. Forgotten ? Never. I can
answer in the name of all my sex. Brave Americans! Your
disinterestedness—your courage—and your constancy, will always be dear to your country, as long as she shall preserve her

virtue.—We know, that at a distance from the theatre of war, if we enjoy any tranquillity, it is the fruit of your watchings—your labours—your dangers. If I live happy in the midst of my family: if my husband cultivates his field and reaps his harvest in peace: if surrounded with my children, I, myself, nourish the youngest, and press it to my bosom, without being afraid of seeing myself separated from it, by a ferocious enemy: if the house in which we dwell—if our barns—our orchards, are safe at the present time from the hands of these incendiaries, it is to you that we owe it. And shall we hesitate to evidence to you our gratitude? Shall we hesitate to wear clothing more simple, and dresses less elegant, while at the price of this small privation we shall deserve your benedictions. Who among us will not renounce with the highest pleasure, those vain ornaments, when she shall consider that the valiant defenders of America will be able to draw some advantages from the money she may have laid out for these, that they may be better defended from the rigours of the seasons; that, after their painful toils, they will receive some extraordinary and unexpected relief, that these presents will be valued by them, at a greater price, when they will have it in their power to say, *this is the offering of the ladies.* The time is arrived to display the same sentiments which animated us at the beginning of the Revolution, when we renounced the use of teas, however agreeable to our taste, rather than receive them from our persecutors; when we made it appear to them, that we placed former necessaries in the rank of superfluities, when our liberties were interested; when our Republican and laborious hands spun the flax and prepared the linen intended for the use of our soldiers. When exiles and fugitives we supported with courage, all the evils which are the concomitants of war, let us not lose a moment—let us be engaged to offer the homage of our gratitude, at the Altar of Military Valor. And you, our brave deliverers—while mercenary slaves combat, to cause you to share with them the irons with which they are loaded—receive with a free hand our offering—the purest which can be presented to your virtue, by

AN AMERICAN WOMAN."

The American Army were rarely supplied with decent clothing, and too frequently suffered from the absolute want of
food ; yet, a devotion to the cause in which they had embarked,
preserved their principles unshaken, and it was rare indeed
that a single murmur was heard. In 1780, the miseries against
which they had to contend were at their height. The cup of
misfortune was filled to an overflow.—The resources of the
country were scarcely adequate to allow a scanty supply of
provision, and the vigilance and activity of the enemy's cruisers on the coast, destroyed every hope of receiving a supply of
clothing from abroad. The safe arrival of a merchant vessel
was considered a miracle. No prospect of relief remained to
the distressed troops, but from the exertions of benevolence
which might induce their fellow-citizens, not immediately in
the field, to open their purses, and from their domestic stores
afford a portion of what might be most conveniently spared.
The patriotism of the inhabitants of the city of Philadelphia,
had already, and on more than one occasion, been put to the
test. Blankets and clothing had been liberally supplied to the
soldiery. But, the complete extinction of trade, had exhausted
whatever might have been possessed of superfluities, and destroyed the ability to bestow what would otherwise have been
tendered with cheerfulness.—The pressure of the times however, required that one more experiment should be made, and
a Matron of Philadelphia,* by a pathetic address to her sex,
very happily accomplished what had previously been deemed
impracticable. Her proposal to make collections among the
citizens of the town and Northern Liberties was adopted, and
immediately carried into effect. A requisition for shirts, was,
by the active exertions of the Committee of Ladies, making the
collections, immediately complied with. Six hundred and
twenty-five pounds in specie, and $200,680 in paper currency,
were rapidly subscribed, and paid into the fund. Great as the
relief must have been to the suffering soldiery, I am altogether
of opinion with a writer in the papers of the day, "that more
beneficial consequences resulted to the cause of liberty." The
idea of favour and affection discovered in the exertion of the

* Mrs. Read.

fair daughters of America, operated like a charm on the soldier's heart ; it gave vigour to exertion, confidence to his hopes of success, and the ultimate certainty of victory and peace. The Ladies of Trenton, in Jersey, imitating the noble example of their Philadelphia friends, were entitled to equal honour. Mrs. Elizabeth Read, the lady of General Joseph Read, the then President of the State, appears to have acted the most conspicuous part, throughout the entire transaction ; unhappily she did not long survive her honourable agency, as it appears from the annexed letter from General Washington to the Committee of Ladies, who presented the patriotic donation to the Army under his command.

New Windsor, Feb. 13th, 1781.

" LADIES,

" The benevolent office which added lustre to the qualities that ornamented your deceased friend, could not have descended to more zealous and more deserving successors.

The contributions of the Association you represent, have exceeded what could have been expected, and the spirit that animated the members of it, entitles them to an equal place, to any that have preceded them in the walk of female patriotism. It embellishes the American character with a new trait, by proving that the love of country is blended with these softer domestic virtues, which have always been allowed to be more particularly their own. You have not acquired admiration in your own country only—it is paid you abroad—and you will learn with pleasure by a part of your sex, where female accomplishments have obtained their highest perfection, and who, from the commencement, have been the patronesses of American liberty. The Army ought not to regret its sacrifices, or its sufferings, when they meet with so flattering a reward, as in the sympathy of your sex, nor can it fear that its interests will be neglected when espoused by advocates as powerful as they are amiable.

I cannot answer to the sentiments which you do me the honour to express for me personally, than that they would more than repay a life devoted to the service of the public, and to testimonies of gratitude to yourselves.

Accept the assurances of the perfect respect and esteem, with which I am, Ladies,

Your most obedient and humble servant,

GEORGE WASHINGTON."

*To Mrs. Francis, Mrs. Hillegas, Mrs. Clarkson,
Mrs. Bache, and Mrs. Blair.—Philadelphia.*

MRS. THOMPSON.

The editor of the *Quarterly Review*, in his first number, says, " Major Garden in his Anecdotes of the Revolution, has assigned a section to the ' Conduct of the Whig Ladies,' and certainly it is not the least engaging of the volume. Mrs. Thompson deserved more than a page in it." The opinion of this gentleman is, in itself, sufficient commendation to establish the claims of Mrs. Thompson to superior merit and patriotic virtue. With the exalted character of her husband, I am well acquainted, and proudly pronounce, that no man served the United States, for so long a period, preserving the unshaken confidence of Congress, and unceasing applause of the nation. With respect to Mrs. Thompson, I am fully satisfied with the Eulogy pronounced on her by her husband; it is sufficient panegyric to entitle her to universal respect: " She never complained of any inconvenience resulting from our situation, in consequence of the war, but did every thing in her power to lighten difficulties and assist me. The business in which I was engaged, I was well aware was too confidential to be entrusted to a secretary or clerk. She aided me with her pen, and the archives of the Revolution contains many interesting pages of her copying."

MRS. ARTHUR PERONNEAU.

Is richly entitled to a place among the most distinguished of our female patriots. The fortitude which she displayed during Provost's invasion, subjected to every species of insult, (her residence being fixed on as the Head Quarters of the British Army,) is highly honourable to her. But in speaking of her merits, I would particularly dwell on her unremitted and affectionate attention to Colonel Hayne, her brother-in-law, during his confinement in prison, and till the day of his death. There was no consolation that could alleviate his sufferings that was not administered. Her sympathy assuaged the afflictions of present calamity, and pious confidence in the justice of a beneficent Deity, encouraged the hope of a crown of martyrdom awaiting his courage and his constancy. On the morning on which he was to die, her son, Mr. Wm. Peronneau, then a youth of twelve years of age, was sent to him, to request that he would spare her the agony of a personal interview which she had not sufficient resolution to support. " Willingly," he replied, " my dear boy. Tell her, that her generous efforts, to save me from an ignominious death, will, to my last hour, be remembered with gratitude, and that my confidence is perfect that we shall meet in a better and happier world."

MRS. BRATTON, OF S. C.

At a period, when an absolute want of arms and ammunition precluded, in a great degree, the possibility of effectual resistance, a small depot of powder was entrusted to Mrs. Bratton, wife of Colonel Bratton, an active officer, serving in the field. The treachery of an individual communicated the important secret to the enemy, and a British detachment was pushed forward to secure so valuable a prize. Mrs. Bratton, informed of their near approach, immediately laid a train of powder from the depot to the spot on which she stood, and seeing no chance of saving her charge blew it up. " Who" exclaimed the irritated officer who led the detachment, " has dared to do this atrocious act? Speak quickly, that they may meet the punishment they deserve." " Know then," said Mrs. B., " 'twas I—and let the consequence be what it will, I glory in having frustrated the mischief contemplated by the merciless enemies of my country."

7

MISS NEWMAN.

THE anecdote which follows, gives strong evidence of the devotion of our Ladies to the cause of America, and the intrepidity with which they supported it :—

An unfortunate whig, flying before a party of the enemy, intent upon his destruction, rushed into the dwelling house of Mr. Trapier, and entering the apartment of Miss Newman, an inmate of the family, exclaimed—" Protect me Madam, or I am lost." " Quickly conceal yourself," replied the lady, " be silent, and rest assured, that I will do all that I can to save you." She had scarcely time to compose herself, before admission was demanded from without, and an officer presenting himself, insisted that the place of concealment to which the fugitive had retired should be immediately pointed out.—" It is little probable," said Miss Newman, " that a soldier, to whom I am probably altogether unknown, would, even under the terrors of death, seek security by intruding himself into my chamber, but, as I am confident that no credit will be given to my assertions, and that the power of search rests with you, its indulgence must necessarily follow. Yet, I trust, from your character as a soldier, and appearance as a gentleman, with the delicacy due to a lady's feelings." The composure so happily assumed, calmed the violence of the party, and the officer, believing that it could alone be exhibited from an entire ignorance of the hiding place of the object of his pursuit, bowed and retired.

MRS. GANNETT, OF SHARON.

The *Dedham Register*, of December, 1820, states : Mrs. Gannett, of Sharon, in this county, presented at Court, her claims for services rendered her country as a Revolutionary Soldier. This extraordinary woman is now in the 62d year of her age. She was about eighteen when the war with Britain commenced. The patriotic sentiments that inspired the heroes of those days, and urged them to battle, found their way to her bosom. The news of the carnage at Lexington had reached her—the sound of the cannon at Bunker's Hill had vibrated in her ears, and increased beyond control her enthusiasm in the cause of liberty. She quitted her home, and the habiliments of her sex, and enlisted in the army under the name of Robert Shirtliffe. For three years she performed the duty of a soldier, and during the whole time enjoyed the confidence of her officers, and unremitted favour by her expertness in exercise, and exemplary good conduct. She served as a volunteer in several hazardous enterprizes, and was twice wounded by musket balls. So well did she contrive to conceal her sex, as to escape all suspicion, till at length a severe wound, which had well nigh closed her earthly campaigns, occasioned the discovery. On her recovery she quitted the army, married, and is now the mother of several children. There were many witnesses in the Court, who recognized her, and were ready to attest to her services.

MRS. STEEL, OF SALISBURY, N. C.

While the army of General Greene was retreating before that of Lord Cornwallis, Dr. Read, who had the charge of the wounded prisoners taken at the Cowpens, was seated in an apartment overlooking the principal street in Salisbury, writing paroles, for such of the British officers as were unable from sickness and debility to proceed further on the route to Virginia, when General Greene, unattended, (his aids-de-camp, being engaged on different services,) rode up to the door, jaded and fatigued, and in fact exhausted to such a degree, as with difficulty to dismount from his horse. "How do you find yourself, my good General," kindly inquired the Doctor. "Wretched beyond measure," replied the General, "without a friend—without money, and destitute even of a companion." "That I deny" said Mrs. Steel, the patriotic land-lady, stepping forward with great alacrity. "That I most positively deny. There exists no cause for such despondency. In me, General, you have a *devoted friend*. Money I have in possession, and *money* you shall have. This young gentleman will not, I am certain, suffer you to be without a *companion* as soon as the humane business about which he is employed is finished. Come with me in the interim, and I will freely give you the money you require." The General followed her into an adjoining apartment, and speedily returned, every pocket filled with gold, which this benevolent and truly patriotic lady had pressed upon him. The name of such a woman should be recorded in letters of gold.

POETICAL ADDRESS.

THE following complimentary address to the Ladies, who so diligently strove to give the comforts of food and clothing to the distressed Soldiery, should not be lost. It contains some good lines and a great deal of excellent sentiment. The encominms bestowed are particularly appropriate:—

All hail, superior Sex—exhalted Fair,
Whose smiles dispel the gloom of dark despair,
Bid the keen anguish of affliction cease,
And to the wounded bosom whisper peace.
Accept the tribute of our warmest praise,
To you the Soldier yields the Patriot's bays;
The Palm of Fame no longer he contests,
Justly decreed to grace the Female breast.
Whilst cherished prejudice remains unarm'd
And e'en pale Envy's into silence charmed—
Freedom no more shall droop her languid head,
Nor dream supine on Sloth's lethargic bed.
No more sit weeping o'er the vet'ran band,
The brave and suff'ring heroes of the land,
Who nobly daring the proud Despot's sway,
Live the admired wonders of the Day.
For to these sons the glorious work renew
Their hopes, their energies, revived by you.
Your gifts more precious in the Soldier's eye
Than all the wealth Potosi's mines supply.
For while his heart with gratitude expands,
Cheer'd by the liberal bounty of your hands,
His pray'rs for you in benedictions rise,
Warm from the soul and grateful to the skies.
Nor there's alone the theme th' Historian fir'd
Shall bless the noble ardor you've inspired.
I want new epithets to adorn his page,
And bid you live admir'd from age to age.
With warm applauses celebrate each name,
Endear your mem'ries and embalm your fame,
For Freedom's Ensign, thus inscribed, shall wave,
"The Patriot Females who their Country saved."

ANON.

PATRIOTS IN THE CIVIL LINE.

ARTHUR MIDDLETON.

I know no man, whose exemplary conduct, throughout the whole progress of the Revolution, deserves more gratefully to be remembered, than that of Arthur Middleton. Possessed of ample fortune, and endowed with talents of the highest order, improved by study, and refined by travelling, he devoted himself with decision to the service of his country. The public, at the commencement of hostility, admiring his zeal, and convinced of his sincerity, placed in him their entire confidence, and never afterwards withdrew it. He served with distinction in the Committee of Five,* expressly appointed by the Provincial Congress to procure the means of defence, superintend the political movements of their fellow-citizens, give energy to the spirit of resistance, and direct with effect inflexible opposition to the encroachments of tyrannical power.† He, on all occasions, advocated the most vigorous measures, clearly evincing that he was not one of those, who shrunk in times of danger from responsibility. Frank and open in temper, he freely uttered the bold conceptions of his ardent spirit, censuring with indignant pride the cautious policy of the timid and irresolute, and expression the highest indignation at the arts of the designing.

His zeal thus manifested, confirming the confidence first reposed in him, he was elected, though scarcely thirty years of age, a member of the Continental Congress of 1775, and thus

---

* Composed of Wm. H. Drayton, Arthur Middleton, Charles Cotesworth Pinckney, William Gibbes, and Edward Weyman.

† The arrest of the Governor. The attachment of the estates of all who deserted the Standard of their Country, &c.

obtained the honour of affixing his signature to the important document, which is regarded by Americans as their richest inheritance. Returning to his native State, new honours awaited him ; he was soon elected to fill the Chair of Government, vacated by the resignation of John Rutledge. The honour, was, however, declined for reasons which proved satisfactory to the public. But, whether in arms for the defence of the city, in exile in St. Augustine, or aiding in the Councils of the Nation—after his release from captivity—we find him with unshaken ardour, by his firmness and undeviating rectitude of principle, giving dignity to the cause he had pledged himself to support.* Shortly after the surrender of Charlestown, (I think it was on the receipt of the news of Lord Cornwallis' victory near Camden, over the army commanded by Gen. Gates,) some of the most influential and zealous Loyalists, considering it a happy opportunity for displaying devotion to their Sovereign, proposed an Address of congratulation to the ruling Authorities, and appointed a committee to tender it to the inhabitants of the garrison, for signatures. Dead to all sense of delicacy, these unfeeling men waited on Mr. Middleton, and prefacing the demand by dwelling on the inability of resistance on the part of the rebels, tendered to him the Address for signature. Virtuous resentment kept him for a moment dumb ! but as soon as indignant passion had sufficiently subsided, to give his feelings utterance—" Begone," he cried, "and from your sight relieve me ! Have you no feeling, wretches, for misfortune, or respect for honest zeal, and faithful service ? Is it in scorn you are come to wreak your malice, on the man who always held your principles and practices in detestation ! or, can you imagine, that after stepping forth in such a cause, and supporting it through every danger and difficulty with steadiness, I will meanly retract, and stamp my name with infamy —Subject myself, not only to the contempt of the world, but the still greater misery of endless and agonizing reproach ? No, no ! it is a mockery that you would add to insult ; and cowardly as well as basely, knowing the restrictions of my pa-

* It was the signing of this Address which caused the confiscation of so many estates at an after period.

role, shield yourselves beneath its protection. This is, to *you*, a day of exaltation, but the hour of retribution *will come* when we shall meet on a more equal footing. Enjoy, meanwhile, your miserable triumph—but, from this room, and my presence, miscreants, retire instantly, and when the liberty is mine to express the just indignation that I feel—*beware!*"

It gives me great satisfaction to add another proof of Mr. Middleton's devotion to his country, communicated subsequently to the completion of the sketch of his character. After his arrest and removal to a ship of war, to be conveyed, with many other distinguished patriots, to St. Augustine, two youths,* under the age of eighteen years, at the period prisoners on parole, anxious to mitigate the sufferings of their relatives, whose sudden separation from their families, and removal to a prison-ship, had deprived them of every comfort, ventured with a few necessaries to repair to the place of their confinement. The pious duty performed, they were about to return to the city, when Mr. Middleton, taking them aside, thus addressed them:—" You see, young gentlemen, the tyranny exercised toward your seniors, whose only crime consists in their unshaken fidelity to their country. Your turn may probably come next. You have already felt the evil hand of oppression bear heavily upon you, and have, doubtless, many and still severer persecutions to endure. Be firm in your attachment to the cause to which you have adhered. Let neither the temptation of promised honours, nor emolument, the fear of personal suffering, the rigor of confinement, nor any oppression that may await you, tempt you to swerve from your duty. Firm in patriotism, bid defiance to every persecution that malice can contrive and power inflict. Great and certain will be your reward. You will find it in the consciousness of well-doing—in the applause of your own hearts—and in the blessings that will follow you, from the gratitude of every virtuous citizen of your country."

It is creditable to the family, that the name of Middleton was ever found opposed to the encroachments of British power.

* Hon. A. Desaussure, since Chancellor of the State, and James Heyward, at a subsequent period a Captain in the Ancient Battalion of Artillery.

Arthur Middleton, grandfather to the subject of this sketch, headed, as Speaker of the Assembly, an opposition which removed the last of the Proprietory Governors. Henry Middleton, his father, was the successor of John Hancock as President of Congress. Arthur Middleton, signed the Declaration of Independence. Henry Middleton, his son, officiated as Governor of the State of South-Carolina, and was one of the most determined opponents of Britain, when that ambitious nation, on a late occasion, sought to disturb the happiness and prosperity of our country. Thomas Middleton, son of an elder branch of the family, residing in England, engaged heartily in the American cause, and was constant in his duty, till his death. John Middleton, who not only enjoyed an estate in Europe, but had the advowson of a church-living of considerable emolument, actuated by a sincere attachment to liberty, crossed the Atlantic to engage in the American service, speedily obtained by his gallantry, a commision in Lee's legion, and possessing the universal esteem of his fellow-citizens, fell a martyr, shortly after the war, to country-fever, sincerely lamented by all who had the happiness of his acquaintance.

THOMAS HEYWARD.

A patriot more resolute in council—more intrepid in the field—more steady in supporting the principles of the Revolution, under the severest afflictions of unmerited persecutions, could not be named than Mr. Heyward.—His was the honour of giving his signature to the instrument that declared America independent. In his military career, he essentially contributed to the defeat of the British on Port Royal Island, and of having repulsed Provost before Charleston. He was actively employed on the lines when Sir Henry Clinton besieged the city, and at its fall became a prisoner to the enemy. The indignities which he then met with were in the extreme disgraceful to the victorious party, but as I have already recorded them in my first series, it appears unnecessary to repeat them. He was distinguished among the patriotic band, who were sent into exile to

8

St. Augustine;—by a playfulness of disposition, which not
only made despondency a stranger to his bosom, but which was
happily displayed in keeping up the spirits of his suffering companions. He wrote songs of humour, and sung them with peculiar glee, and although little can be said in favour of their
poetical merit, yet, in his satirical remarks on false patriotism,*
and animadversions on the foibles of the tyrants, who oppressed them, he not only amused his companions, and imparted to them a portion of his own cheerfulness, but caused them
to check unavailing murmers, and to look forward with confidence, to the happy termination of their sufferings, and the perfection of their country's glory and happiness. I am inclined
to give great credit to Mr. Heyward, for his clear and early
perceptions of the happy results that would follow, from bold
and unremitted exertions against the encroachments of Britain.
On his return from Congress, his father, who was not altogether
as sanguine in his calculations of success as he had been, said
to him, "My son, in declaring America independent, you have
adopted a very bold measure, and I am inclined to think, with
precipitation, since undisciplined militia, and we have no other
troops, can never resist the attacks of brave and well-trained
regulars. We shall, inevitably, be beaten." "Granted," said
Mr. H. "What, then, are we to do?" rejoined his father.
"Raise a new army, and keep up the contest." "What! to
be again beaten." "Most certainly, and the same result may

---

* An individual, who delighted to proclaim the purity of his patriotic principles, and
the steadiness with which he considered his honour as pledged to support them, was frequently heard to say, "Should it ever be my misfortune to fall into the hands of the
enemy, though subjected to every species of insult, and goaded by every variety of oppression—though imprisonment and chains, the dungeon's gloom and rack's tortures he
my lot—though, in time, my legs and arms should be severed from my body, *the Honest
Trunk*, that remained, would still be true and faithful, to the cause of liberty, and of my
country." It is a dangerous thing for men to place too great confidence in their own
strength, or to boast their ability to encounter and overcome difficulty, before the hour
of trial has overtaken them. The town, in which this firm and intrepid patriot resided,
being closely besieged and taken, to the astonishment of the community, he was among
the first of the capitulants, to recant his opinions, and to solicit with humility, forgiveness for his political errors, promising, if the ruling authorities would condescend to
grant him protection, that he would sin no more. His dereliction of principle, met with
its proper reward, for, remaining in Charleston, after its evacuation by the British Garrison, he never walked the streets, or ventured to show his face in public, before his ears
were saluted by the mockery of every school-boy, exclaiming, "there goes *the Honest
Trunk*." How fares it with the unshaken patriot, and steady friend of his country.

follow, over and over again, but, by dint of perseverance, we shall become reconciled to the evils of war, and daily acquiring experience, in the military art, ultimately wrest the palm of victory from the enemy, and repay, with ten-fold energy, the defeats received at their hands." "He will tell you, in mockery of one of our country phrases, that it is only necessary for them to show themselves, for our untutored bands, *'to split and squander.'*" But, let us patiently wait the results of steady opposition, and then we shall see, 'on whose side the laughers will be.' Remember, too, Sir, that every success that follows their exertions, will necessarily be attended with a loss of men, and that recruits can only be obtained by bringing them across the Atlantic, and that at an enormous expense, while the temporary defeat of our armies, produces no material evil, in this respect; the very men, who fled with precipitation from the field to-day, being ready, and with the hope of getting rid of the disgrace, will resume a hostile position to morrow." I repeat, that this happy view of the eventful occurrences of the war, just entered upon, was highly creditable to the discernment of Mr. Heyward, more especially as the results proved them to be altogether correct, in every portion of the Union, before the termination of the war. They, who had triumphantly over-run the Jerseys, Virginia, the Carolinas, and Georgia, being ultimately, (unless when under the immediate protection of their shipping they indulged in pedatory expeditions,) confined to the narrow limits of the cities of New-York, Savannah, and Charleston. Mr. Heyward, after the conclusion of the war, was elected a Judge, and as a civil officer, from his clear, unbiassed decisions, gave increase to the reputation acquired by his zeal and activity in the field, when acting in a military capacity.

JUDGE BEE.

The claim, of this respectable citizen, to Revolutionary celebrity, is unquestionable. Through every period of the struggle for Independence, he adhered to the cause of his country, with ardent zeal and unshaken constancy, and that he performed his duty with advantage to it, must appear evident, from the situations of trust and honour to which he was raised by the voice of his fellow-citizens. The duties of Member of the Assembly, Speaker of the House of Representatives, Member of the Privy Council, Judge of the State Courts, Member of the Council of Safety, Lieutenant Governor, Member of Congress, and, finally, Judge of the District, were discharged by him with distinguished credit and applause. He was mild in disposition, amiable and conciliating in his manners, and from his liberal feelings, afforded, to the last hour of his life, a genuine portrait of Carolina hospitality. One trait of his character, merits particular notice :—He had suffered much by the war —his property had been in the hands of the enemy, and had not escaped the cupidity of many of them, noted for their rapacity in plundering, but his resentments ceased when they had no longer power to injure. Their departure from our shores extinguished his resentments. The unfortunate, who, by the errors of their conduct, had incurred the displeasure and resentment of their countrymen, found in him a steady and powerful advocate; he pitied their weaknesses, and anxiously strove to remove their disqualifications, and to reconcile them to their country and to themselves; and, I doubt, if a single instance can be brought forward, where pardon was solicited, where he did not plead the cause of the offending party. A bill for the encouragement of Literature and Science, introduced into the House of Representatives, immediately after the evacuation of Charleston, originated *with him*. Whilst every society, having a view and tendency to promote the diffusion of knowledge, met in him a strenuous supporter; we may have seen in the distinguished personages of society, men of more brilliant character, but with none better entitled to the esteem and veneration of his countrymen, than Judge Bee.

RICHARD HUTSON.

Mr. Hutson, at the commencement of the Revolutionary war, was possessed of a large and unencumbered estate, the whole of which he sold, the better to aid his country in her arduous struggle for liberty, by placing the product in the funds. His zeal did him honour, but proved his ruin; the depreciation of Continental money leaving him in poverty and indigence. His talents, however, (it was all he had to give,) were unceasingly devoted to the public welfare. As a soldier, lawyer, legislator, long as the war continued, he conducted himself with such propriety, that immediately after its conclusion, he was chosen one of the *Three Chancellors* of the State. And on the incorporation of the city of Charleston, chosen its first Intendant. In this last station his conduct was exemplary. Many turbulent spirits appeared intent to disturb the peace of Society; mobs were raised—some mischief done, and a great deal contemplated, but by zeal, activity and firmness, he put down all irregularities, and preserved the tranquility of the city. Mr. H. was an excellent scholar, and it is said completely master of seven different languages. He was mild and amiable in disposition, and to his friends and relations, one of the most kindhearted and affectionate of human beings. They were inexpressibly dear to him, but he loved his country still more, as the sacrifice of his property clearly evinces. In confirmation of what I have alleged of his patriotism, I have it in my power to state, that General C. C. Pinckney, often declared that he did not know an individual to whom Carolina was as much indebted, for active zeal, and perpetual sacrifices in her service. Praise from such a man, is sufficient eulogy, without the addition of a single sentence of commendation from my pen. For the penetration of the General, in estimating character, was singularly correct, and his uprightness, when called on for the delivery of his sentiments upon it, would have caused him rather to lose his life, than utter a falsehood, or bestow the meed of praise on one, who had not richly deserved it. I have omitted to mention, that he was one of the exiles who was sent to St. Augustine; the British were too well convinced of the influence of his precepts and example, to suffer him to remain in Charleston. Their grand object was to make converts, and to induce the weak and wavering to enlist under their banners; pretexts were therefore found for depriving the true or steady patriots, who were within their power, of the benefits of the capitulation under which they had become prisoners, and to treat them, not as *gentlemen*, but as felons, who were destitute of all sense of honour, and not entitled to the slightest share of pity or indulgence.   At St. Augustine, they would be comparatively harmless, and thither they were sent.

AMERICAN OFFICERS—MILITARY AND NAVAL.

GENERAL GEORGE WASHINGTON.

It may appear extraordinary, that in giving sketches of the characters of the heroes and patriots, the most distinguished in the Revolutionary war, that I have never particularly noticed, the man above all others, pre-eminent in talent and in virtue; and whose clear perceptions, in a great measure, directed the energies of the rest. It cannot be doubted, but that my allusion is to the immortal WASHINGTON, who, by universal consent, has been acknowledged, not only the pride and glory of his country, but an honour to the human race. But, already, all that relates to his character and conduct, in private life, the field, or cabinet, has been detailed by our historians so fully and skilfully, that nothing that I could say, would afford an additional claim to celebrity. I think, however, that my admiration of his character has been sufficiently elucidated throughout the whole of my Anecdotes. The expression of General Gates, made in the presence of Dr. Read,* gives a striking instance of the goodness of his heart—his generous inclination to forgive injuries, (for he was well-apprized of all the secret intrigues of Gates, to injure him, and dispossess him of command,) his sympathy in the heart-rending afflictions that had fallen on his family. The humanity exercised toward Sir Charles Asgill, (fully detailed in the present series of Anecdotes, although most ungenerously requited;) his pity for his sufferings, is not less creditable to his feelings. The delicate rebuke given to the gentlemen of his family, whose boisterous mirth

* Pages 34 and 35, First Series.

disturbed the repose of a wounded officer,* at once declares his discretion and keen sense of propriety. The friendly visit to Colonel Wasson, his solicitude for his recovery, and grateful acknowledgment of his services, his worth, and usefulness to the army, excite high admiration. The anecdote related in the present series, of his temperance, and happy mode adopted, to quiet the discontents of the army, remonstrating by a deputation of field officers, against the badness and scarcity of their rations. The delicacy of his feeling towards the foe he had subdued,† do him the highest honour. With high admiration I view his clear discernment of character, in the employment of Lt. Colonel Jo. LAURENS, as a negotiator; of WAYNE, for effecting a hazardous enterprize by a *coup de main*—of HARRY LEE and M'LEAN, as vigilant and active partizans—of WILLIAM WASHINGTON, as a soldier, well calculated to execute services the most daring—of STEUBEN, to perfect discipline in the army —of LA FAYETTE, to command where caution was necessary to avoid a regular action with a foe greatly superior to him in numbers, and, at the same time, when spirit was necessary to keep him in check,—and, finally, his choice of GREENE, to take command of the Southern army, to restore their courage and rekindle their expiring efforts. All of which notices proclaim a genius of superior cast; a penetration rarely equalled. Of neglect, then, I shall scarcely be accused, where such proof has been given, that no man, in a higher degree, knew how justly to appreciate the exalted talents and virtues of the immortal WASHINGTON.

PENNSYLVANIA OFFICERS.

Biographical sketches of the superior officers of the Pennsylvania line, have been so skilfully drawn by their immediate friends and contemporaries, that any additional notice of their services from my pen, might appear superfluous. To the Generals, BUTLER, WALTER STUART, SINCLAIR and WAYNE, I had the honour to be personally known, and was immediately

* Page 393, First Series. † Page 394, First Series.

under the command of the last, when, at the period of its evacuation by the British, he took possession of Charleston. General Butler, was, from the commencement to the end of his military career, considered as an officer of superior talent. Much of the celebrity of Morgan's Rifle Regiment, (declared by General Burgoyne, to be the finest marksmen in the world,) was derived from his skill in training, and example in leading them to victory. WALTER STUART, an Irishman by birth, was enthusiastically devoted to the cause of liberty, and supported it with the characteristic bravery of his countrymen. SINCLAIR, possessed all the requisite qualities for command, and had he been properly supported, would never have suffered the British to boast the triumphs, which crowned the early progress of their army, led on by Burgoyne. WAYNE, was a complete soldier, delighting in enterprize, intelligent in all emergencies in the perception of his duties, intrepid in the discharge of them. Such, indeed, was his chivalrous gallantry, that anticipations of success were always cherished by the soldiers under his command, and led by *Mad Anthony*, (the name by which he was designated,) the order to engage the enemy, was considered as a prelude to victory. Bold in all his efforts to compel his enemy to submission, his moderation in the hour of triumph, was exemplary. At *Stoney Point*, as soon as resistance ceased, there was an end to slaughter, and it certainly redounds to his honour, when the hope of conquest was relinquished by the British, and a disposition was manifested to quit our shores, that he was opposed to the unnecessary waste of lives, and preferring negotiation to actual hostility, acceded to the proposals of the Generals CLARKE and LESLIE, and took possession, both of Savannah and Charleston, without the loss of a man.

GENERAL WILLIAM IRVINE.

I now beg leave to notice an officer of peculiar merit, whose claims to applause have never, in my opinion, been sufficiently appreciated. I allude to General WM. IRVINE, a native of Ireland. He received while a student at Trinity College, Dublin,

through the influence of a lady of quality, a commission in a
Regiment of Dragoons, but meeting with injustice in a contest
with a brother officer, relative to rank, he gave in his resignation, and assiduously applying himself to the medical profession,
was appointed a Surgeon in the Navy, and served in that capacity till the peace of 1763. A strong attachment to America, contracted in the course of service, causing him to emigrate
to Pennsylvania, in 1764, he settled at Carlisle, and with great
advantage to the public, and credit to himself, engaged in the
practice of physic. The contest with Great Britain commenc-
ing in 1774, he engaged with ardent zeal, in the service of his
adopted country, and after having essentially contributed to
the dissemination of pure and genuine principles of liberty
among his fellow-citizens, and inducing Pennsylvania cordially
to join the Union, for the support of the just rights of America,
accepted the command of a Regiment, and marched at its head
into Canada. An unsuccessful attack upon the van of the enemy's army, at the village of Trois Revieres, was the occasion of
his absence for a considerable period, from military service;
for, the corps in which he served, under General Thompson,
being defeated, he became a prisoner. The conduct of Sir Guy
Carlton, to the captive officers of the American army, has been
generally and deservedly applauded, but towards Colonel Irvine, it was inflexibly severe, whether from caprice, or from an
opinion, that, he, who had once served under the British banners, should, under no circumstances, have drawn his sword in
opposition to them, is uncertain. But, the indulgences granted
to others, were denied to him; his side-arms were taken from
him, and so many impediments thrown in the way of his liberation, that it was not till the year 1778, that his exchange could
be effected.

He then took the command of the 2d Pennsylvania Brigade, and rendered essential service at the head of it, till detached in 1781, to Pittsburg, to protect it, being charged at the
same time with the defence of the North-Western frontier,
threatened by the British and Indians, with invasion. His
prudence, while engaged in this important service, cannot be
too highly commended. By his moderation he effectually

quieted the differences existing between the States of Virginia and Pennsylvania, and by attention to the discipline of corps which he commanded, and indefatigable care in collecting provision, military stores, and every requisite for defence, in all probability saved Pittsburg from a similar calamity to that which fell so heavily on the settlement at Wyoming. He was subsequently highly instrumental in bringing to reason the disaffected in what has been called the Whiskey Insurrection, and finally closed his life of usefulness, in 1804, in the sixty-third year of his age, performing, at that period, the duties of Superintendent of Military Stores, and acting as President of the State Society of Cincinnati. I shall only add, in confirmation of my own sentiments, the opinion of the General, forwarded to me from the pen of an inestimable friend,* who enjoyed his confidence, and served for several years in his family, as his aid-de-camp. " In spite of the indignities heaped on him by General Carlton, he never failed to speak with high commendation of his military talents, declaring, that although we owed much to the blunders of their Generals, in the achievement of our Independence, we owed still more to the British Minister, who superceded Carlton in command, giving the conduct of the war to a leader of very inferior ability. To General Washington, I knew him to be devoted, and on the best grounds assert, that the reciprocity of opinion on the part of the Commander-in-chief, was as flattering to General Irvine, as he could have wished. . In Council, his sentiments were generally approved and considered as orthodox. He was not a man of many words, but he wrote well. In his habits and manners, he appeared *forbidding* and austere, but under that exterior possessed unbounded benevolence, and executed all the duties of his station as Commander of the 2d Pennsylvania Brigade, with unremitted industry, and to the satisfaction of all serving under his authority. The simplicity of his fare, (while the tables of other Generals were abundantly supplied) contenting himself with bread and milk, or, perchance, a salt herring, was believed by many to proceed from extreme parsimony, but I knew the contrary. He was the declared friend of temper-

* Major Gibbon, of Richmond.

ance, and well knew, that example in recommending it, would
have far greater influence than precept, superadded to which,
it was his decided opinion, that the fare of the officer should
not be of a superior quality to that of the soldier, with equal
ardour, contending for the liberties of his country.   In short,
should I become his biographer, I would proclaim him, in addition to the possession of great strength of mind—brave,
patriotic, persevering, liberal, and humane.   Need there more
be said, to portray the distinguished Soldier? Certainly not."

ALLEN M'LEAN, OF DELAWARE.

I know of no individual, of his rank in the army, who engaged in such a variety of perilous adventures, or who, so invariably brought them to a happy issue, as Allen M'Lean. A brief statement of his services, will best demonstrate his merits as a soldier, and claims to public favour as a zealous and inflexible patriot. At the commencement of the Revolution, he possessed a comfortable independency, holding in the city of Philadelphia, in houses and lots, property, equal in value to fifteen thousand dollars, the whole of which he sacrificed in the service of his country. At the very commencement of hostilities, we find him stepping forward as a volunteer. Persuaded, from the ardent temper and strong prejudices of Lord Dunmore, that an apppeal to arms would speedily occur in Virginia, he particularly directed his attention to that quarter, and witnessed the repulse of the British at the Great Bridge. This early dawn of success giving increase to his military ardour, his utmost efforts were exerted to fit himself for command, and in 1775, a lieutenant's commission was presented to him, in a Militia Regiment, commanded by the Hon. Cæsar Rodney, of Delaware. In 1776, he joined the army under General Washington, near New-York. The battle of Long Island speedily occurring, afforded an opportunity, which he eagerly embraced to acquire distinction. Observing the exposed situation of a British party, he obtained from Lord Sterling the aid of a small detachment from the Delaware Regiment, made a lieutenant and eighteen privates, prisoners, and though surrounded by the enemy, led them off in safety. He was present at the battle of the White Plains—witnessed the capture of the Hessians at Trenton, and at Princeton, by his good conduct and exemplary gallantry, so particularly attracted the attention of General Washington, as to be immediately appointed to a

Captaincy in a Continental Regiment.—Sent into Delaware to recruit, he speedily rejoined the army with ninety-four men, raised at his own expense, every shilling of the bounty-money being drawn from his pocket.

On the march of the British army from the head of Elk, the particular duty assigned him was, to annoy them, which he did with effect, but at the expense of a lieutenant killed, and a considerable number of his men. Philadelphia being possessed by the British, after the battles of Brandywine and German-town, the important duty was assigned to him by the Commander-in-chief, to watch the movements of the enemy, to protect the whig inhabitants, (as much as practicable) residing near the lines, and to prevent the disaffected from carrying supplies to the city. The results evinced the prudence of the measure. M'Lean was vigilant and active, and remarkably prudent, though possessed of the most dauntless intrepidity. On the very first night of service, he took three spies, fifteen British soldiers who had quitted the city in search of plunder, and twelve tories, carrying in supplies to the enemy. A discovery of the highest importance immediately followed. On the 3d of December, 1777, intelligence was communicated to him by a female, who, under some frivolous pretext, had passed the British lines, "that the enemy were to leave the city on the ensuing night, in hopes to surprise the Camp of General Washington, at White Marsh." Prompt in communicating this information to the Commander-in-chief, his immediate care was to intercept the progress of the foe. A position was accordingly taken near Germantown ; when, so well-directed a fire was opened upon their front, that the British, supposing a considerable force at hand, desisted in the attempt to proceed further, and immediately formed a line of battle. Recovering, however, from their first surprize, they moved on in three columns, and about day-dawn appeared in front of the American encampment.—For two days they occupied this position, when Gen. Morgan, driving in their pickets on the right, and General Washington, making arrangements for a general attack, they struck their tents and precipitately returned to the city.

The service rendered to the Marquis De La Fayette, in the

following month of May, was no less important. Entrusted by
General Washington with a separate command, that aspiring
soldier had taken post at Barren Hill Church. A traitor giving intelligence of his situation to General Howe, the Generals,
Grant and Erskine, with five thousand picked men, were ordered to gain his rear; while General Grey, marched forward
to attack him in front, and prevent his crossing the Schuylkill.
The capture of two Grenadiers brought to M'Lean the first intelligence of the movement, which left no doubt on his mind,
but that to strike at the Marquis, was the object of the expedition. Grant, accomplished his object, but finding his troops
much fatigued by a night-march of twenty miles in a few
hours, thought proper to wait the approach of Grey. M'Lean
reached Barren Hill about day-break, and imparted his appre-
hensions to General La Fayette, who could scarcely credit the
report; but it was speedily confirmed from many quarters, and
particularly by Captain Stone, of the Militia, who, hearing the
British as they passed his dwelling, leaped from a window, and
ran naked across the country towards Barren Hill, till perfectly
exhausted, he met a friend, who took up the report and speedily conveyed it to the Marquis. There was no time for deliberation. The army was immediately led across the river at
Marston's Ford. But, had Grant, in the first instance, pushed
forward and occupied the strong grounds at the Ford, it is presumable that the command of the Marquis, not half as numerous as his own, must have surrendered, or been destroyed.

While General Washington lay at Valley Forge, M'Lean
passed into the State of Delaware by his order, and rendered
essential service by collecting supplies for the army, which
could not otherwise have been obtained. Resuming his command before Philadelphia, in 1778, he never failed to vex and
harrass the enemy, till they evacuated the city, and hanging
on their rear at the moment of embarkation, made one captain,
a provost-marshall, three sergeants, two corporals, and thirty-
four privates, prisoners. During their retreat through the
Jerseys, he never ceased to annoy them, and by his activity at
Monmouth, gave increase to his well-earned reputation.

He served under Major Lee, both at the reduction of Paulus

Hook, at which last named post, fifty prisoners were taken, and a gang of counterfeiters, who had imitated the Continental money, so exactly, that at the treasury the false could not be distinguished from the genuine bills.

His conduct at the reduction of Stoney Point, deserves to be more particularly mentioned. Being ordered with a flag of truce, to conduct a Mrs. Smith to the post at Stoney Point, that lady having quitted it for the purpose of carrying some necessaries to her sons in New-York; he assumed the appearance of a simple countryman, and being politely received by the British officers, did not fail, while conversing with them, to examine with a soldier's eye, the strength of the position, and the points at which it would be assailable, with the best prospects of success. His split shirt, and rifle accoutrements, appear to have particularly attracted the attention of a young officer, who said to him—" Well Captain, what do you think of our fortress—is it strong enough to keep Mister Washington out?" "I know nothing of these matters," replied M'Lean, " I am but a woodsman, and can only use my rifle; but, I guess the General (not Mister Washington, if you please) would be likely to think a bit, before he would run his head against such works as these. If I was a General, sure I am that I would not attempt to take it, though I had fifty thousand men."
—" And if," rejoined the officer, " General Washington, since you insist on his being styled *General*, should ever have the presumption to attempt it, he will have cause to rue his rashness, for this post is the Gibralter of America, and defended by British valour, must be deemed impregnable."—" No doubt, no doubt," replied M'Lean, " but, trust me, we are not such dolts as to attempt impossibilities, so that, as far as we are concerned, you may sleep in security." On the night subsequent to this conversation, the post was attacked and carried. Colonel M'Lean assured me, that when recognized by the officer, it would have been impossible to give a just idea of his surprise and confusion. The folly of his former boasting, appeared to rush on his mind with a peculiarly distressing effect, and he hastily retired, overwhelmed with shame and mortification.

In June, 1781, entrusted with despatches of the highest importance by General Washington, to the Count de Grasse, he took the command of the Marines on board of the ship Congress, mounting twenty guns, and one hundred and forty men, and arrived at Cape Français in July; there he found the Count holding a Council of War, the object of which was, to fix on proper measures for an immediate attack on the Island of Jamaica. But, before any definite arrangements could be made, the presence of M'Lean was called for, that he might be examined relative to the preparations made in America, for a combined attack by the Allies and American army, on the British force in the Chesapeake. To the interrogatories proposed, he gave such satisfactory answers, and developed such cheering prospects of success, that he was informed by the Count, soon as the Council broke up, that he would immediately proceed to America, and act as circumstances might require, until the hurricane months should have passed over. Returning home with this pleasing intelligence, the Congress fell in with the British sloop of war Savage, of twenty guns, and one hundred and forty men, engaged her, and after a desperate action of five glasses, succeeded in capturing her. The Congress lost her boatswain, carpenter, two master's mates, and fifteen of her crew; the Savage, her sailing master, two midshipmen, and twenty-five of her crew. The victory, so honourable to the flag of the United States, was attributed, in a great degree, to, the constant and well-directed fire of the marines.

He was next ordered to take post near Sandy Hook, and being furnished with a barge to visit Long Island, was directed to communicate with persons from New-York, and having received from them the private signals of the British fleet sailing for the Chesapeake, for the relief of Lord Cornwallis, returned to the Jersey shore, embarked in a pilot-boat, and delivered them safely to the Count de Grasse. He then took his station on the lines before York, till the garrison surrendered.

I could detail many other anecdotes relative to M'Lean, but what I have already written, is, in my estimation, amply sufficient to prove, that he was much relied on for his judgment, courage and integrity; that he retained the confidence of the

10

Commander-in-chief, the Board of War, and the General officers he acted with, to the end; that he was in all the principal
battles fought in the States of New-York, New-Jersey, Pennsylvania, Maryland, and Virginia; that he served his country
faithfully on water as well as land; and, that although frequently contending with superior numbers, and exposed to
every peril, he still extricated himself from difficulty, by the
superiority of his courage and presence of mind, with distinguished eclat.

I annex a copy of the Certificate of Service, presented to
him at the conclusion of the war, by General Washington:—

"Allen M'Lean, Esq., was appointed a Captain, in one of
the additional Continental Regiments of foot, in 1777, and by
activity and industry, soon joined the army, with a Free Company. He commanded a party of observation, under my instructions, until July, 1779, when he was annexed, by a resolution of the Honourable Continental Congress, to Major Lee's
Legion, to command the Infantry. From the certificate, which
Major M'Lean is possessed of, it appears that he was early active in the cause of his country, and from the time of his joining the Continental army, I can testify, that he distinguished
himself highly, as a brave and enterprising officer. Previously
to the siege of York, he was employed to watch the motions of
the British army, near New-York, as well as in Virginia, and
was entrusted with despatches of the first importance to His
Excellency, Count De Grasse, which commission he executed
with great celerity, and was afterwards very serviceable in reconnoitering and bringing intelligence of the strength and disposition of the British army and fleet in the Chesapeake.

Given under my hand and seal, at Rocky Hill, near Princeton, November 4th, 1783.

GEORGE WASHINGTON."

On one occasion, doing duty near the British lines, finding
his horse greatly fatigued, and himself much in want of rest
and refreshment, he was retiring towards Germantown, when
the enemy's cavalry appeared in view, and advancing with a

rapidity that threatened to cut off the possibility of a retreat. The Commander of the British forces, perceiving that pursuit as a body would impede the celerity of movement, essential to success, selected two of his best mounted troopers, and ordered them to continue the chase, and use every possible exertion to make him their prisoner. The first of these approaching very near, called to M'Lean by name, and ordered him to surrender, but he, preserving his presence of mind, drew forth the only pistol he possessed, and leveling it with effect, laid his adversary prostrate in the dust. The second now coming up, was, in turn, eagerly charged, and being struck from his horse by the butt-end of the pistol that had disabled his companion, was incapacitated from using any further exertion. M'Lean, continuing his route, sought shelter in a swamp, where he remained in security, till the evening afforded him an opportunity of rejoining his command."

My wish on the present occasion is, to speak only of the occurrences of the Revolutionary war, but I have in my possession, an interesting memoir from the pen of Colonel M'Lean, relative to the proceedings of the Army before Washington, when taken and pillaged by Ross, the British General, that fills me both with grief and astonishment. Briefly to notice it, the Colonel says :—

" All was confusion—nothing like spirit—nothing like subordination—universal complaint for the want of food, the Militia going off in every direction to seek it. Men, badly armed, being, in many instances, without flints in their muskets, and so completely without discipline, as to exhibit a far greater resemblance to an armed mob, than an organized army. I most religiously believe, that if I had been at the head of three hundred men, such as I led on to the attack of Paulus Hook, or such as I had under my command, during the war of our Independence, I should have defeated General Ross, when he pressed General Winder over the Eastern Branch. Confident I am, that the enemy would never have reached Washington, and America been spared the disgrace of beholding the British triumphantly possessing the Capitol."

GENERAL ANDREW PICKENS.

The following instance of cool and deliberate heroism, is given as illustrative of the military character of one of our distinguished partizan officers—General Andrew Pickens. Owing to the rude and wild state of the back country, in the Revolution, our Heroes of that section of country have not been as honourably known to posterity as they deserve. I am gratified that it has been put in our power, by the politeness of a friend, on whose information the most complete reliance can be placed, to throw some light upon the obscurity of those times and transactions.

" In September, 1776, General Andrew Pickens, being then a Major, belonged to an army of two thousand men, composed of Regulars and Militia, commanded by Colonel Williamson, which was sent on an expedition against the Cherokees, who had been instigated by the British emissaries, to wage a war of extermination against the frontier inhabitants of the country, now composing Abbeville, Laurens and Spartanburgh Districts. When this army had proceeded into the Indian country, as far as the upper part of what is now Pickens District, it was halted for a day or two, either for rest or to gain intelligence. During this time, Major Pickens obtained permission to take twenty-five choice men, to scout and reconnoitre the adjacent country. He had not proceeded more than two miles, when, early in the morning, after crossing a stream, now called Little River, in passing through an old Indian field, along the margin of the stream, which was covered with a thick grass, four or five feet high, more than two hundred Indians, painted for war in the most hideous manner, were seen rushing down the point of a ridge, directly upon them, with their guns swinging in their left hands, and their tomahawks raised in their right : their leader animating and exhorting them not to fire a gun, but to tomahawk the white men, for they were but a handful. Brennan, a half-breed, was one of

the twenty-five, and he, understanding them, told what they
said. Major Pickens and all his party were on foot, and he,
as well as every other, had his trusty rifle. He ordered his
men not to fire until he did, to take deliberate aim, and fire
two at a time in succession, and to fall in the grass and load.
Brennan was by his side in front, and when the Indian chief
approached within about twenty-five yards, he and Brennan
fired, and two Indians fell; the fire of his other men was in
succession, as directed, and equally effective. This invincible
firmness, in so small a band, astonished and struck terror into
the savage ranks, and they immediately recoiled upon each
other, dropped their tomahawks, and resorting to their guns,
gradually fell back, and were picked out at leisure by the steady
and unerring aim of this small band of firm Militia. After
the first or second fire, Brennan was shot down. But few
were killed or wounded of the whites; if they had not been
brave men, and true, not one would have escaped. Major
Pickens, in loading in a hurry, soon choaked his gun, when he
picked up Brennan's and continued to use it while the Indians
were in reach. How many of them were killed, could not be
known, as the Indians, in those times, always carried off their
dead, whenever they could, to prevent their enemies from acquiring their savage trophy, the scalp; but, it was believed a
great number were killed, in proportion to the number of com-
batants opposed to them.

During the action, one of the men observed that there was
a constant firing from behind a tree-root, and watching his opportunity when its occupant had to expose himself to take aim,
shot him in the head, and when one of his comrades had taken
up the dead body, and was making off with it, shot him also,
with as much coolness, as if he was shooting at a target, and
they fell, one upon the other. The firing was heard at Williamson's camp, when Major Pickens' youngest brother, Joseph,
(killed at the Siege of '96,) who was a Captain, immediately
summoned his followers, and hastened to his brother's assistance. But, before he could reach him, the Indians were beaten
back, dispersing, and fleeing to the neighbouring mountains.
Captain Pickens, was a man of great animation and zeal, and

was often bold and loud in his abuse and crimination of men,
who were tardy in their movements for the deliverance of his
brother, accusing them of cowardice, but Major Pickens paci-
fied and rebuked him for his warmth."

BOYD'S DEFEAT AT KETTLE CREEK.

The successes of the British in Georgia, had great influence
in arousing the hostile spirit of the tories in the upper districts
of South-Carolina, which had been smothered, but not extinguished. They had been encouraged to embody themselves,
and cross the Savannah River, where they were told, that by
uniting themselves to the British Regulars, so great a superiority of force would be obtained, as to render resistance to the
Royal Government abortive, and extinguish every symptom of
rebellion. A Colonel Boyd, a man of some influence, who had
been effectually tampered with, undertook to be their leader,
and actually marched some hundreds of them across the Chero-
kee Ford, into Georgia. A more motly crew were never collected, being composed chiefly of persons distinguished by their
crimes, and infinitely more anxious to plunder, and appropriate whatever of value they could lay their hands on to their
own use, than to promote the good of the cause, and the interests of the Monarch, they professed to admire and to serve.
Colonel Pickens, always on the alert, collected about three
hundred well-affected Militia, and immediately followed in pursuit. They had gained little or no advantage when he overtook them at Kettle Creek, where he attacked them with such
impetuosity that after losing forty men, they became panic-
struck, and fled in every direction, leaving the whigs in possession of the battle-ground, and all the spoils collected on their
march. Had they successfully joined their allies, there is no
saying where the mischief would have ended; for, there was
an abundance of inflammable material left behind, and the example of Boyd, might speedily have been followed up, on a
more extensive scale of revolt, and with more decided effect.
The promptitude of Col. Pickens, therefore, in collecting men,

and bringing the contest to so successful an issue, does him great honour, and cannot be too highly commended. The prisoners taken were numerous, and seventy of them were condemned to die as traitors, but mercy tempered the exercise of rigid justice, and five only were executed.

COLONEL I. E. HOWARD, OF MARYLAND.

When I first heard of the death of Colonel Howard, I was strongly impressed with the idea, that in the notice taken of his services, in my first series of Anecdotes, I had in no degree bestowed commendation adequate to his merits. But, in recording the single expression of General Greene, " *Howard is as good an officer as the world affords,*" I am satisfied that additional encomium is altogether unnecessary, and that although I might write volumes, I could not increase his claims to celebrity. It will not, however, be amiss to state, that he engaged in the military service of his country, at a very early period after the war had commenced, and while attached to the Northern army, was present at the battles of the White Plains, of Germantown, and of Monmouth. But, it was in the Campaigns of the South, that his valour and skill attained the acme of perfection. His was the honour of having first broken the line of the British army at the Cowpens, by a charge of the bayonet; a mode of warfare employed on many future occasions, and always with the most perfect success. Nor were his services less conspicuous in the brilliant actions which followed at Guildford, Hobkirk's Hill, and Eutaw, in the last of which, he was so severely wounded, as to be compelled to retire from the army. Colonel Howard, at the conclusion of the war, received every honourable appointment in the Civil Establishment, that the gratitude of his State could bestow. When the aggressions of France occasioned a new army to be raised for the security of our country, he received from the Commander-in-chief, General Washington, who knew how to appreciate his talents, the appointment of Brigadier General, which, however,

he was compelled to decline. I shall conclude this short notice of him, by giving a brief account of the battle of the Cowpens, in conformity to his own statement. His words are
these :—

"The Militia were formed in front of me, and the moment
the British formed their line, they shouted and made a great
noise to intimidate, and rushed with bayonets upon the Militia, who had not time, especially the riflemen, to fire a second
shot. The militia fell into our rear, and a part of them on my
right flank, where they afterwards renewed the action. The
British advanced until my regiment commenced firing. I soon
observed, as I had but about three hundred and fifty men, and
the British about eight hundred, that their line extended much
farther than mine, particularly on my right, where they were
pressing forward to gain my flank. To protect it, I ordered
the company on my right to change its front, so as to oppose
the enemy on that flank. Whether my orders were not well
understood, or whether it proceeded from any other cause, in
attempting this movement, some disorder ensued in this company, which rather fell back than faced, as I wished them.
The rest of the line, expecting that a retreat was ordered, faced
about and retreated, but in perfect order. This retreat was
accidental, but was very fortunate, as we thereby were extricated from the enemy. As soon as the word was given to halt,
and face-about, the line was perfectly formed in a moment.
The enemy pressed upon us in rather disorder, expecting the
fate of the day was decided. They were, by this time, within
thirty yards of us, with two field-pieces; my men, with uncommon coolness, gave them an unexpected and deadly fire.
Observing that this fire occasioned some disorder in them, I
ordered a charge, which was executed so promptly, that they
never recovered. When I came up to the two pieces of artillery, which we took, I saw some of my men going to bayonet
the man who had the match. He refused to surrender it, and
I believe he would have suffered himself to have been bayonetted, if I had not rescued him, rather than give up his
match."

One Anecdote I would add, which, though not Revolutionary, merits to be recorded :—

After the disasters at Washington, when the city of Baltimore was threatened, with the immediate horrors of war, a suggestion was made in the Committee of Vigilance and Safety, of which Colonel Howard was a member, that it would be the best course for the city to capitulate. He indignantly opposed the very mention of the proposition, declaring, that though the bulk of his property was at stake, and he had four sons in the field, he would rather behold his property reduced to ashes, and his sons weltering in their blood, than witness the adoption of a measure, so disgraceful to the honour and character of his country.

In the House of Representatives, of the State of South-Carolina, January 25, 1828.

E. S. Davis, of Abbeville, introduced the following preamble and resolutions which were unanimously adopted :—

It becomes a grateful people to cherish and perpetuate the memory of the brave and the good, to remember with gratitude their services, and to profit by their bright examples.

The heroic band of the Revolution, who fought that we might enjoy peace, and conquered that we might inherit freedom, deserve the highest place in the grateful affections of a free people.

Amongst the master-spirits who battled for independence, we are to remember with veneration the late patriotic and venerable Colonel John Eager Howard. His illustrious name is to be found in the history of his country's sufferings and the annals of his country's triumphs. In the day of peril and of doubt, when the result was hid in clouds—when the rocking of the battlements was heard from Bunker's Hill to the plains of Savannah—when danger was every where, and when death mingled in the conflict of the warrior, Howard still clave to the fortunes of the struggling republic. Of all the characters whom the days of trial brought forth, few are

11

equal, none more extraordinary. He was his country's common friend, and his country owes him one common unextinguishable debt of gratitude. South-Carolina, with whose history his name is identified, is proud to acknowledge the obligation.

In the chivalrous and hazardous operations of General Greene in South-Carolina, Colonel Howard was one of his most efficient officers.

On a certain occasion, that experienced General declared, that Howard merited a monument of gold, no less than Roman or Grecian heroes. At the battle of the Cowpens, says Lee, he seized the critical moment, and turned the fortune of the day.

At Eutaw, and at Camden, he led the intrepid Maryland line to battle and to glory.

But, in the course of human mortality, it has pleased the Almighty to remove him from among the few remaining associates of his youth.

Resolved, Therefore, that it was with feelings of profound sorrow and regret, that South-Carolina received the melancholy intelligence of the death of Colonel John Eager Howard, of Maryland.

Resolved, That the state of South-Carolina can never forget the distinguished services of the deceased.

Resolved, That the Governor be requested to transmit a copy of these proceedings to the Governor of Maryland, and to the family of the late Colonel Howard.

JOSHUA BARNEY, OF MARYLAND.

It gives me peculiar pleasure to present to the view of my readers, a sketch of the achievements of a Revolutionary officer, whose ardent zeal, unremitted exertions, and exemplary intrepidity, during our struggle for freedom, were rarely equalled, and certainly never surpassed. Examples of heroic valour are more efficacious in promoting the desire to emulate them, than the most animating and encouraging precepts, and there is little doubt in my mind, but that the cheering influences of magnanimous daring, displayed by several young and inexperienced officers, in our first contest with Britain, had their full effect in exalting, to the sublimity which it attained, the reputation of our Naval Heroes in the last. For undaunted spirit—patience under the pressure of adverse fortune—active enterprize in the pursuit of honour, and a happy talent to profit by favourable occurrences to attain it, I never knew a man, who had superior claim to Captain Barney. A brief sketch (and I can only make it a brief one, from the quantity and variety of matter relative to our Revolution, in possession) will afford ample proof, of the correctness of my assertion. Shewing an ardent desire to engage in a seafaring life, his father, (though reluctantly) indulged his wishes, and in 1771, being at Alicant, and having the command of a ship, though but seventeen years of age, he engaged in the Transport service, and witnessed the disastrous defeat of the Spanish forces under Count O'Reilly, before Algiers. Returning to America in October, he first heard of the battles of Lexington and Bunker's Hill, and of the general excitement against Great Britain. Zealous for the honour of his country, and ambitious for fame, our young sailor immediately attached himself to a fleet fitting out at Philadelphia, under the command of Commodore Hopkins, and was received as Master's Mate, on board the Hornet, sloop of ten guns. The American flag having been sent to Baltimore for this vessel, was first displayed to the admiring citizens by Barney, who attaching it to a staff, and beating up for recruits, in *one day*, engaged an entire crew. In November, the Hornet joined the fleet, consisting of eight vessels, carrying one hundred and eighteen guns, and sailed for New-Providence. The town, fort and shipping, having surrendered without opposition, all articles of a warlike nature were seized, and being received on board, the fleet returned to the Delaware. On the voyage, the Hornet fell in with the Tender of the Roebuck, which vessel being ignorant of her character, immediately ran alongside.—"I was in the act of running out one of our guns," says Barney, "and held a match in my hand ready to fire, when our Captain, who was of a religious turn, and opposed

to the shedding of blood, commanded me to desist, and the
Tender escaped.—This hypocritical fellow, however, as if
ashamed of his conduct, kept below, and taking command, I
carried the vessel safely to Philadelphia." Changing to the
Wasp, he next convoyed the vessel, carrying Dr. Franklin to
France; off the coast, and, on returning, being closely pressed
by the British cruisers Roebuck and Liverpool, gladly united
his force to that of the Lexington and Saratoga, brigs, laying
in the Cape May channel, under the command of Captains
Barry and Weeks. A vessel appearing off, the enemy chased
and drove her on shore. The American boats were immediately sent to assist her in landing her cargo, consisting of arms
and powder; but, it appearing impossible, from the near approach of the British, to effect their purpose; loose powder
was, by Barney's order, scattered in the vessel's hold, and a
brand of fire, judiciously placed in a sail contiguous to it, she
was scarcely boarded before she blew up, and every man was
destroyed. Barney, in the Wasp, now took the Tender, that
had escaped the Hornet, and arrived safely in Philadelphia,
and received for his services, from that distinguished patriot,
Robert Morris, President of the Marine Committee, a commission, as Lieutenant in the Navy of the United States. Being
appointed to the Sachem sloop, commanded by Captain Joshua
Robinson, he sailed on a cruise, and falling in with a Letter-of-
Marque Brig, after a smart action of two hours, succeeded in
capturing her. Her cargo was rum, and she had on board a
fine turtle, intended for Lord North, which the captors, with
peculiar pleasure, presented to Mr. Morris. In this action,
every officer in the Sachem was either killed or wounded, except Barney and the Captain. Captain Robinson, was now
removed to the Andrew Doria, of fourteen guns, and Barney
appointed his Lieutenant. Cruising off St. Eustatia, in company with the Lexington, they saluted the Fort, but had the
mortification to learn, that the Commandant, for returning the
compliment, was suspended and recalled to Holland, at the request of the British Government. Returning homewards with
a cargo of powder and arms, they fell in with, and captured a
sloop called the Race-Horse, attached to Admiral Parker's

fleet, which, under the command of a Lieutenant in the Navy, had been fitted out with a picked crew, expressly for the purpose of taking the Doria. A Snow was the next capture, and Barney put on board as Prize-master; but, adverse fortune speedily overtook him, and he was compelled to surrender to the Perseus, of twenty guns, commanded by Captain G. K. Elphiston. Two seaman on board the Snow, who had agreed to do duty on condition of being allowed a share of prize-money, refusing, on being chased by the Perseus, to fulfil their engagement, Barney shot the instigator for mutiny, through the shoulder, who calling loudly for revenge, was cruelly mortified to find Captain Elphiston, not only justifying, but applauding the act. It is a pleasure to speak of this excellent officer, and generous enemy, whose humanity towards his prisoners was conspicuous throughout the war, and who, on this occasion, gave so decided a proof of his justice and regard for discipline. Nor was this the only instance of his strictly correct conduct, for the Purser of the ship, having, without provocation, struck Barney, the blow was returned, and the aggressor knocked over a quarter-deck gun, and precipitated down the hatchway; nor was this the extent of his punishment, for refusing, when ordered by Captain E. to ask pardon for so unjustifiable an outrage, he was immediately put under an arrest, and left in that condition when Barney quitted the ship.

Being, after some time, exchanged, he assisted with a Flotilla, under Com. Hazlewood, in defence of Mud Fort, in the Delaware, till every gun but *one* being dismounted, it was judged expedient, to burn the larger vessels, and in boats and gallies to retire in the night up the Delaware; which, was happily effected, having previously witnessed the destruction of the Augusta 64, and Merlin, Sloop of War, belonging to the British squadron. Barney was now ordered to join the Virginia Frigate, Captain James Nicholson, laying in the Chesapeake, but was speedily put in command of a Tender, to watch the enemy, and report any favourable opportunity that might occur for the Frigate getting to sea. On one of his cruises, being chased by a vessel of ten guns, he saw a sloop from Baltimore, with which he had been in company the day before, and made towards her to give intelligence of the approach of an enemy, but on nearing her, was saluted with a fire of musquetry and ordered to strike; recovered from his first surprise, he tacked and stood for them, speedily overpowered her crew, retook the sloop, captured the barge which had taken her, and returned triumphant to Baltimore. The kindness with which he treated his prisoners, produced on this occasion a complimentary letter from Capt. Squires, who commanded in the Bay, with a suitable present. It was an act of justice very frequently merited by the American officers, but rarely paid by their opponents. I would, if possible, pass over the disgraceful business of the loss of the Virginia Frigate, which Barney now joined. Had *his* advice been followed, she had been run on shore, when overpowered, and her crew saved from captivity; but her *Captain quitting* her, subordination ceased, her crew got drunk, plundered the store and slop rooms, and then surrendered. Captain Caldwell, of the Emerald, taking possession of her, with exemplary politeness, invited Barney to share his cabin, and to all the other prisoners, behaved with such pointed attention, that the British seamen nick-named him "*the Rebel Captain.*"

This generous conduct was so much appreciated by Barney, who was frequently permitted to go on shore, that having given it publicity, Patrick Henry, the Governor of Virginia, sent a pressing invitation to Captain C. to join a hunting-party, which, circumstances compelling him to refuse, supplies of every kind, were abundantly sent from the shore, as a tribute due to his humanity. Barney, is now to appear in a new light. Removed on board of the St. Albans, of sixty-four guns, with other prisoners, amounting to upwards of five hundred, this vessel, and the remainder of the squadron, sailed for New-York. Barney, perceiving that she was feebly manned, conceived a project, which, had it not been communicated to a traitor, would probably have resulted in one of the most brilliant achievements recorded in Naval History. His aim was to capture the ship. The inducements to attempt it were strong and flattering. The American officers occupied the gun-room, where nearly all the small arms were deposited.

The plan was well digested; every man had his station allotted to him, and his peculiar duty clearly pointed out. Barney and two others, were to seize the Captain in his Cabin, and secure the private signals, by means of which he would have the power, without difficulty, to capture the whole fleet. Every thing was prepared—the hour fixed on, and each man impatiently waiting the signal to begin—when, half an hour before the time, a guard came and removed the small arms, and double sentinels placed in every direction, though not a word was spoken. Barney dined the next day with Captain Onslow, but no symptom of suspicion was betrayed, nor a word uttered to give an idea of alarm. During the whole passage, the same caution was observed. Arriving at length within Sandy Hook, Barney was again invited to dine in the cabin, when the Captain, with a significant smile, observed, " and so Barney, you were delegated to seize on me. I hope, however, you did not meditate any personal violence; your scheme was certainly plausible, and might have succeeded, had your secret not been betrayed to me in time by one of your *new friends*—a *Frenchman.*" For this act of villainy, the rascal obtained his liberty, and Barney was transferred to a prison-ship. Admiral Gambier, arriving shortly after, and finding Barney the only Continental officer in confinement, not only had him removed to his own ship, (the Ardent, of sixty-four guns,) but with distinguished humanity, did every thing within the reach of his ability, to ameliorate the sufferings of the unfortunates left behind him. He even indulged Barney to go on shore at pleasure, a favour, which, on one occasion, had nearly cost him his life; for, passing a street where a fire raged, the surrounding mob thought fit to regard him as an incendiary, and were about throwing him in the flames, when the name of the Admiral being mentioned, as his friend and protector, reason overpowered prejudice, and he was dismissed. Exchanged for a Lieutenant of the Mermaid Frigate, which had been driven on shore by the French fleet, Barney returned to Baltimore, and finding no public vessel there, joined his old commander, Captain Robinson, and sailed in a private ship for Bordeaux. Being but badly manned, ill-armed, and almost destitute of ammu-

nition, the wish was to avoid an action; but, speedily a British
ship run along-side, and though beaten off with loss, renewed
her attacks, hanging on her quarters, and giving infinite an-
noyance, until Barney, hoisting a long three-pounder on her
quarter-deck, and cutting a stearn port, by a fortunate discharge of grape and landgrage, to which a crow-bar was added,
so completely carried away her foretack, and all her weather-
shrouds, that her commander was obliged to wear ship to save
his foremast.   In this condition they left her, and proceeded on
their voyage, having but two men wounded, while their adversary, which proved to be the Rose Bud, of eighteen guns, lost,
in killed and wounded, forty-seven men.

Arrived at Bordeaux, they shipped a crew of seventy men,
and mounted eighteen six-pounders, sailed for Philadelphia,
and captured on the passage a Letter-of-Marque, of equal force,
killing seventeen men, and wounding others, brought her safely
into port.   Having now a considerable share of prize-money, he
thought that an excellent opportunity offered of making his for
tune by speculation, and set out for Baltimore with that intention, but found to his mortification, on reaching that city, that
his trunk had been opened and stripped of its contents, and that
he was left without a single dollar.   Barney's was not a heart
to give way to despondency, or unnecessarily to lament an in-
curable evil; he, therefore, immediately joined the Saratoga,
Captain Young, of fifteen nine-pounders, and sailing on a
crnize, made prize of a ship, shewing twenty, but carrying only
twelve guns.   I have now to mention an action, in which Barney bore a distinguished part.   Falling in with a ship, carrying thirty-two guns and seventy men, a brig of fourteen guns,
and a smaller one of four guns, from Jamaica, bound to New-
York, the Saratoga laid the ship along-side, and Barney, at the
head of fifty men, boarding her, drove her crew below, and
struck her colours, and then, with his prize, pursuing the brig
with four guns, captured her also; the larger one of fourteen,
in the interim, surrendering to the Saratoga.   These vessels
contained a cargo of nineteen hundred hogsheads of rum, then
selling at Philadelphia, at three dollars per gallon, and every
man considered his fortune as made; but, falling in with a

British squadron at the mouth of the Delaware, all the prizes were retaken; the Saratoga herself, with great difficulty getting off. Barney was taken on board the *Intrepid*, and in her Commander, *Anthony James Malloy*, met with a tyrant, who, by his barbarity, disgraced both his country and his profession, keeping his prisoner for several days on the poop, in a severe snow-storm, without permitting him to enjoy the comforts of clothes or bedding. Arrived at New-York, he was put on board the Yarmouth, of seventy-four guns, and sent to England. On this voyage, the situation of the prisoners was truly deplorable, confined in a miserable dungeon for fifty-three days, without light, and breathing only noxious air; the ravages of disease carried off eleven of their number, who all died raving mad. On his arrival at Plymouth, Barney could scarcely stand, but being removed to a prison-ship, and from thence to the mill-prison, he speedily recovered both his strength and activity. Detected in an attempt to escape from the last, he was ironed, and confined for thirty days to a dungeon. This did not, however, deter him from making a new effort to regain his liberty, and in the undress of a British officer, being favoured by a friendly centinel, who had served in America, and been well-treated there; he did so effectually. Repairing to the house of a friend, he was kindly received and secreted. Throughout the whole of Britain, at that time, there were many of the inhabitants, who not only applauded the resistance of America, but sincerely wished success to her arms. Their sentiments were delivered without fear, and their purses opened with liberality, and who never, though the penalty of high treason was attached to the offence, failed to aid the prisoners who had escaped from their dungeons, and to facilitate by their utmost efforts, their return to their friends and country. Disguised as a fisherman, and accompanied by *Colonel Wm. Richardson* and *Dr. Henderson*, of Maryland, who were prisoners at Plymouth, Barney now attempted to cross the channel, and gain the French coast, but on the passage was captured and brought back to port. Escaping from his captors, he again sought the dwelling of his friend, and having provided himself with a fashionable suit of clothes, set out in a

12

post-chaise and four, for Exeter; at the gate the chaise was stopped by a centinel, who said, that he was ordered to keep a sharp look-out for sailors and deserters, but awed by the genteel appearance of Barney, he speedily closed the door and retired. Passing from Exeter to Bristol, and from thence to London, he speedily proceeded on to Margate, and embarked for Ostend. The weather on the voyage was bad, and Barney, discovering among the passengers a lady, who suffered exceedingly from sea-sickness, bestowed on her his entire attention. To him it was a fortunate meeting. Arrived in port, she invited him to her hotel, and finding that he was travelling the same route with herself, insisted on his taking a seat in her carriage to Brussels.

The Emperor Joseph was on a visit incog. to this part of his dominions, and being introduced to him by his female friend, Barney was gratified by a long and interesting interview. The lady, who was an Italian, now set out for Turin, and Barney proceeded on his course to Holland. Here he joined the South-Carolina, commanded by Com. Gillon, which he pronounced the finest Frigate in the world, and sailing North-about, after the capture of a Privateer, put into Corunna, when, finding that Gillon had no intention of returning immediately to America, he sailed in a privateer bound for Beverly, and arrived in safety. The command of a ship of twenty guns was now offered him, but fortunately refused; since, arriving at Philadelphia, through the influence of his steady friend, Robert Morris, he was appointed to the command of the Hyder-Alli, of sixteen guns and one hundred and ten men, and speedily achieved a victory that crowned him with imperishable honour and renown. His particular duty was to convoy vessels going to sea, and to protect them from refugee boats that swarmed in the river Delaware. Lying on one occasion at Cape May, waiting for a wind, that his convoy might put to sea, he saw two ships and a brig making towards him, the Convoy was ordered up the Bay, Barney keeping constantly in their rear. One ship and the brig came into the same channel in which he was, the other ship took another course, with a view to head him. The brig first came up, delivered her broad-side and passed on; the ship next approached within pistol-shot, when a well-directed broad-side was poured into her from the Hyder-Alli; the enemy closed, and came near on board; Barney, crossing her hawser, got entangled in her fore-rigging, and keeping her in a raking position, by an irresistible fire of great guns and small arms, in twenty-six minutes brought down her colours. The brig, perceiving the ship's misfortune, run on shore, to avoid a similar fate. Barney and his prize proceeded up the Bay. The captured vessel, proved to be the General Monk, mounting twenty nine-pounders and one hundred and thirty-six men, commanded by Captain Rogers. She lost twenty men killed and thirty-three wounded; among the first, the First Lieutenant, Purser, Doctor, Boatswain, and Gunner: among the last, the Captain, and every other officer, one Midshipman alone, excepted. The Hyder-Alli, had four men killed and eleven wounded. The Legislature of Pennsylvania, on this occasion, voted to Captain Barney, a gold-headed sword, which was presented to him by the Governor of the State. The General Monk was sold, and being bought in by Government, Barney had the honour of being appointed to command her. Ordered with despatches to the French and Spanish Admirals in the West Indies, he performed the duty with uncommon expedition—captured one prize, and took on board sixty thousand dollars, in specie, belonging to private individuals, and arrived safely in Philadelphia, being absent only thirty-five days on his voyage. Returning up the Bay, he had the good fortune to fall in with a fleet of refugee boats, sunk one, having sixty men on board, and retook their prizes, five in number, without loss. He was now ordered to France, having on board the Secretary of the French Ambassador, carrying despatches to his Government. His fair fame and high reputation for chivalric valour, had preceded him, and on his being presented at Court, the most gracious reception was given by the Monarch, and grateful compliments bestowed by the surrounding Courtiers. In January, 1783, being entrusted with a large sum in specie, and despatches for Congress, by Dr. Franklin, he sailed in the ship General Washington, under a passport from the King of England, but did not

arrive in America until March. Preliminary Articles of
Peace, had been signed before his departure from France,
which he exultingly declared, but it was not till he had delivered the money which he had in charge, and produced his passport, and shewed a letter from Dr. Franklin, communicating
the happy event, that belief was given to his assertions. The
joy was universal. The Liberty of America appeared established upon the firmest basis, and peace was regarded as the
certain harbinger of prosperity and happiness. The activity
of Barney remained undiminished; he made several voyages
in the service of the United States, but there was no longer a
call for the display of that enterprize and valour, that so particularly characterized the man. From 1775 to 1783, his may
be considered a life of incessant service, peculiarly honourable
to himself, and useful to his country. I have confined myself
to facts, well authenticated, and yet, I have little doubt, but
that my narrative will be considered by many more a romance
than a real story. He was the first of the Naval officers of our
country, who engaged in the service—he was the last to quit
it. He was the favourite of the nation—the terror of its enemies—the friend of his professional associates, and of every virtuous citizen. I could not say more in his praise, though I
were to write volumes.

Documents have been furnished me, to show, that during
the late war with Great Britain, age had not damped the ardour of his youthful fire, and that the patriotic virtue, which
had first induced him to draw his sword, to obtain his country's
freedom, was as prompt to wield it, in defence of her established rights. But, to enter into details, would be foreign to my
purpose, as I wish to confine myself to Anecdotes, connected
with our Revolutionary war. I, nevertheless, flatter myself,
that it will be clearly understood, that Com. Barney was, ever,
in my eyes, a *Hero*, unbounded in his affection to his country,
and ready at her call, to risk his fortune and his life, to prove
his perfect devotion to her interests. I cannot, however, avoid
stating, and on the very best authority, that had but a few ardent spirits like his own been present when the British ap-

peared before Washington, America had never suffered the disgrace of having the Seat of Government captured and destroyed, with scarcely an effort made for its defence.

Sometime after the commencement of the French Revolution, Barney served with distinguished credit under the Tricoloured Flag. Being taken by the British, and carried into Jamaica, indefatigable pains were taken to fix on him the crime of piracy, and to condemn him as a lawless bandit. The attempt, however, failed, and ample was the retribution which followed the insult, for he confidently assured a friend, on whose statement I can depend, that subsequently cruising in the British channel, he had captured property to the amount of one hundred and fifty thousand dollars.

LIEUT. JOHN MAYRANT.

I have in my first series, recorded the services of more than one Naval hero, but in my notice of the unparalleled conflict which occurred between the Bon Homme Richard and the Serapis, have neglected to mention the distinguished intrepidity of a highly meritorious officer, Lieut. John Mayrant. I had the happiness of being in habits of strict intimacy with this gentleman in the days of our youth. I prized his friendship too highly to have neglected him through design, and flatter myself, that by introducing him on the present occasion, to the public, some reparation will be made, and my inadvertency excused.

Mr. John Mayrant, while yet a mere boy, serving under Paul Jones, as a Midshipman, obtained distinguished honour. His conduct during the battle had evinced extraordinary coolness and resolution, and when, as it drew near to a conclusion, an order was given to board, he was the first to leap into the enemy's vessel, and while animating his followers by his example to that display of heroism, that speedily secured the palm of victory, was severely wounded. His exertions, however, though checked, were not altogether paralyzed, and till the colours of the Serapis, were struck, refusing to quit the deck, he displayed a calm intrepidity, which, even to a veteran, accustomed to such scenes, would have given an additional laurel. Shortly after this action, Mr. Mayrant changed his ship, being appointed a Lieutenant on board the South-Carolina frigate, commanded by Commodore Gillon. His services in this situation, gave great increase to his reputation, not his bravery only, but his humanity also, being exercised with peculiar eclat. I will give, in the words in which it came into my hands, a communication which I have every reason to believe perfectly correct:—

"As the frigate South-Carolina, commanded by Com. Gillon, was cruising between the Bahama Islands and the Florida Keys, it happened one night, (Lieut John Mayrant being officer of the deck,) that he was ordered to keep a good look-out and the lead a-going; and a Midshipman with a night-glass was placed at each quarter. About two hours before day, the one stationed on the starboard announced, that he perceived a rock: upon a nearer inspection, it proved to be a fleet, and on drawing still nearer, a Jamaica fleet. About 4, A. M. the frigate was close aboard four of them and another ship was to be seen at about five miles to windward; to secure the whole prize was now the object of the Commodore, but one, which there was no possibility of attaining without having recourse to artifice; and, after a hasty consultation with his officers, the following line of conduct was determined on:—In the first place, the Frigate having British colours flying, hailed the four ships nearest to her, ordering them to heave to, and promising to send a boat aboard of them. Lieutenant Mayrant, was then ordered to take a barge, and with twenty-four choice men and about four or five marines,(himself, as well as the marines) being all in British uniform, to make for the furthest vessel; he did so, and when arrived under her stern, and rounding upon her quarter, in answer to the Captain's inquiry, as to what boat that was, replied that it was the barge of the D'Artois, commanded by Captain M'Bride; the Captain ordered him to keep off, threatening to fire into him. Lieutenant Mayrant, in return, commanded him to heave a rope immediately, and asking if he would dare to fire into his Majesty's boat, ordered his men to pull along side; on hearing this, the British ship, without further dispute hove a rope, and manned her sides; such being the ceremony usually observed in receiving an officer. Lieutenant Mayrant immediately stept on board, having previously ordered his men not to follow, but on receiving a concerted signal; the Captain received him with great politeness, and the usual inquiries having been made and answered, Lieutenant Mayrant desired to see his papers, in order to examine them: No sooner had the Captain gone below, in the search of them, than Lieutenant Mayrant's men, receiving the expected signal, stept on board to the number of twenty, all armed with cutlasses, and having pistols concealed under their jackets. The Captain having returned, Lient. Mayrant, after examining the papers, inquired how many men he had on board, and on his replying that there were forty, ordered him to take his papers and twenty men, and to go with them on board of the Frigate; he replied 'why, surely Sir, you do not mean to impress my men at sea.' Lient. M. replied, 'certainly not, but Captain M'Bride, being a very particular man, wishes to examine the men and papers himself.' The Captain still hesitated, upon which Lient. Mayrant reiterating his order, made a sign to his men to draw their sabres, on perceiving which, the Captain, not choosing to risk a contest, obeyed Lient. M.; ordered him to row off, while he would undertake to carry the ship down to the Frigate. As soon as the Captain was fairly off, Lient. M. ordering the remainder of the crew below, reversed the British colours. At which sight, the consternation of the Captain, who, from the barge, was a spectator of what passed, may be better conceived than expressed; he declared it to be a damned Yankee trick; but, the deception was discovered too late, and he found himself obliged to go on board of the Frigate: by this means, Commodore Gillon was enabled to capture the whole fleet, consisting of five Jamaica men, heavily laden with sugar and rum.

Lieutenant Mayrant, remained in possession of the ship, which he had been instrumental in taking, and which proved to be the Nelly, Captain Noble, with fourteen eighteen-pound carronades, compliment of forty men, bound from Jamaica to Glasgow, laden with four hundred hhds. of sugar, and one hundred of rum. After having been in command of her two or three days, and sailing in the Gulf Stream, it happened that a man, whom he had ordered to heave the lead, was, by a pitch of the ship, thrown from the main chains, overboard: the ship was immediately hove to, and several coops and chests thrown overboard to him; it was then attempted to lower the boats to his relief, but on trial, they were found to have remained dry so long, as to be unfit for the purpose. Lient. M. was then obliged to make sail on the ship, as she had drifted considera-

bly from having her sails aback; he then, by making a stretch
and a tack, succeeded in coming up with the man, and brought
him to about twenty feet on his weather-bow. Lieut. M. then
called to some of his men to jump overboard and carry him a
rope: but, though none refused, they hesitated so long, that
Lieut. Mayrant, perceiving that there was no time to be lost,
as the ship was drifting fast, took hold of the end of a rope himself, jumped overboard, and swimming up to the man, put it in
his hands. The ship being at this time in the Gulf Stream,
with all her sails aback, drifted so rapidly, that Lieut. M. and
the sailor were drawn, at the end of the rope, considerably under water; the sailor now letting go the rope, clung round
Lieut. M's neck, who found himself obliged also to let go his
hold, in order to extricate himself, which he succeeded in doing; as soon as they rose to the surface, they both then swam
to a hen-coop, of which they took hold, one at each end; on
this coop they remained three hours and a half. Meanwhile, the
Frigate South-Carolina, perceiving the Nelly, (which was about
ten miles distant from her,) wearing and stearing, and putting
out signals of distress, concluded that the prisoners on board
had risen and retaken the ship, but on making up to her, was
informed that Lieut. M. and one of the men were overboard;
the direction being pointed out, in which they were last seen,
they were soon after perceived by a man at the mast-head of
the Frigate, who pointed them out; the Frigate, as soon as she
came near them, lowered five boats, which spread themselves,
and about half an hour before dark, Lieut. M. and the sailor
were taken up by one of them; the sea was, at this time running so high, that the boats could not discern them, and the
sun was down."

Lieutenant Mayrant, at a subsequent period, opened a House
of Rendezvous at Philadelphia, for the enlistment of Sailors,
which was kept by the mother of the sailor, whose life he had
preserved. On this occasion, his humanity met with an ample reward, for the gratified parent, feeling influenced by the
recollection of the service rendered her, plead the cause of her
benefactor with such persuasive eloquence, portraying his char-

13

acter in such terms, as the sailor's friend—the brave supporter
of his country's rights, and above all, his readiness to risk his
life to save that of a fellow tar, that he had only to select the
followers he wished for, every man who had listened to her, being anxious to enlist under his banners.

BRITISH OFFICERS.

In my first series of Anecdotes, I have spoken freely of the characters and conduct of the British Officers, who served in Carolina, endeavouring, without prejudice or partiality, to

"Give the palm, or shake the rod as justice turned the scale."

I certainly omitted to speak well of an officer, entitled to high commendation, and consider it a duty, as far as in my power, to repair my error.

LIEUT. COLONEL MAITLAND, OF THE SEVENTY-FIRST REGIMENT.

I cannot imagine how the merits of so distinguished an officer escaped my notice in my first publication, since it has been my invariable aim to give to every individual, who was entitled to it, a just meed of praise, and no one more richly deserved it than Colonel Maitland. To consummate intrepidity, he united a humanity towards the unfortunate, that gave additional grace to every laurel that he won. His valour at Stono, was highly conspicuous, and caused the ultimate discomfiture of General Lincoln's army, which, in the early part of the engagement had been triumphantly successful. But, in no instance was greater benefit rendered to the government which he served, than in his indefatigable efforts to relieve his associates in arms shut up in Savannah, and closely invested by the combined forces of France and America. Deep and universal despondency, prevailed within the Garrison, and the only deliberation was, how to render submission as little disgraceful as possible. Every avenue by which the approach of Colonel Maitland and his Highlanders could be looked for, was closed; yet, by unconquerable industry, he discovered an obscure creek, but little navigated, and by dint of persevering

exertion, dragging his boats through it, reached the Garrison
before the time allowed for deliberation had expired. Entering the Council Chamber, where discussions were carrying on,
he is said to have approached with hurried step, the table, and
striking the hilt of his claymore against it, to have exclaimed,
"the man who utters a syllable recommending surrender,
makes me his decided enemy; it is necessary that either *he* or
I, should fall." So resolute a speech, at a moment so critical,
produced the happiest effect on the minds of all. Hope and
courage regained their influence in every mind—each individual repaired to his post, with alacrity and confidence; the
terms offered by the besiegers were rejected, and the town
was saved.

DAVID CAMPBELL, OF THE SIXTY-FOURTH REGIMENT.

Of inferior grade, but of the most pure and honourable principles, this excellent officer and benevolent man, settled in Carolina after the war, and lived for many years, beloved and
admired by the entire community. At the period of his death,
the following obituary notice of him, appeared in our public
prints:—

"Died, recently, after a lingering and severe illness, David
Campbell, Esq. of St. Bartholomew's Parish, in the sixty-
second year of his age. He served with distinguished reputation during the war of our Revolution, as a Captain in the
British 63d Regiment. He landed on our shores as an enemy,
but to his honour, it must forever redound, that as far as it was
in his power to prevent it, misfortune was never aggravated by
insult, An advantage gained by the army in which he served,
was but a prelude to the exercise of every liberal attention towards his opponents, that could mitigate the severity of the
reverses they had experienced. His purse was as open as his
heart, and although as a Subaltern, his means could not have
been great, yet, proportioned to his ability, its contents were

never withheld from the unfortunate, but bestowed with such unaffected tenderness, as to render every benevolence doubly valuable. In battle brave—in victory generous and humane. A higher character need not be given of him, to render Carolinians, who admired his virtues while living, feelingly to join in sympathy, with his surviving family, and to lament the stroke of fate, which deprives them of a member, so worthy of their most exalted love, and admiration. At the conclusion of the war, Captain Campbell left the British service, married and settled in Carolina, and by uniformly supporting the character of an amiable man, and useful citizen, commanded the esteem of all who knew him."

I cannot here but repeat, with grateful respect, the names of Brigadier General Clarke, Colonels Webster, Campbell of the 71st, Small, and M'Arthur, the Majors Majoribanks, Money, and M'Elroth, and the officers of the Staff, M'Mahon and Buck. In Carolina, the names of Roberts and Lloyd, D. Campbell, Graham, and Torriano, of the 63d and 64th Regiments. Of the Lieut. Colonels, St. George and Fox; Captains Steward of the Guards, Wynyard, of the 33d, M'Kenzie, and Charles Morris, whose attention to their suffering schoolfellows and early friends, never knew abatement, are always held in the highest veneration. While eternal ignominy rests on the names of Rawdon, Weymess, Cochran, Provost, and Baird, with a multitude of others, who, with less power, had equally strong inclinations to oppress and to destroy.

THE M'KENZIES.

I HAVE mentioned in my First Series of Anecdotes, that when our gallant countryman Major Pinckney, received a wound at Gates' defeat, which placed him in the hands of the enemy, the generous feelings of an old school-fellow, Captain Charles Barrington M'Kenzie, of the 71st British Regiment, under the blessing of Heaven, saved his valuable life.* This brave sol-

* Vide First Series, page 287.

dier had a brother in the Naval service, whose misfortune it
was to be taken, in a small Sloop of War which he commanded,
by the Amazon, of thirty-six guns, Capt. La Peyronse. The
Frenchman had, immediately before the action, conveyed Major Pinckney, on board the Languedoc, Count D'Estaign, wishing to have an officer of intelligence and conversant in the
French language, near his person. This circumstance being
incidentally mentioned, and the fact established, that Major P.
was present, with the combined forces, before Savannah. Captain M'Kenzie, confident that war had not weakened the force
of early friendship, said to the gallant Frenchman, tendering
his services, "let me have the pleasure of receiving the comforts
I stand in need of from *Tom Pinckney;* let him but know
what my wishes are, and he will not fail to have them fully
gratified." How cruel the recollection, that the wild ambition
of a corrupt and arrogant administration, should have attempted
to estrange hearts united by such congeniality of sentiments,
from each other.

MR. JAMES SIMPSON.

It should forever redound to the honour of **Mr. Simpson,** the
first President of the Board of Police, that the only use which
he ever made of his power and influence, was to mitigate the
sufferings of the unfortunate, and by generous attention, to free
them from every taint of political animosity, and to reconcile
them to a government which they appeared unable to resist.
Nor is less credit due to him from his clear perception of the
policy which should have been adopted in the hour of triumphant success. He constantly opposed every arbitrary decree
that issued from the higher authorities, and warned them of the
inevitable results that would follow the tyrannical measures
pursued. Wearied out by his fruitless efforts to promote a reconciliation, and check the progress of oppression on the one
hand, and of discontent on the other, he resigned the exalted
station which he held, and retired to Europe; foreboding the
disasters and disgrace, that were speedily to obscure the glory

of Britain. To add to the misery of the country, Sir Egerton Leigh, was appointed to succeed him. What sort of man he was, may be seen by a reference to my First Series, page 225.

— ♦ —

CAPTAIN M'MAHON.

The interesting Anecdote which follows, relative to the ardent and firm attachment of General C. C. Pinckney, to the American cause, was communicated to me by Captain M'Mahon, an officer of distinguished merit. His liberality towards the unfortunate, while Charleston was held by the British, proves that he was a man of pure and honourable sentiments, and it is to be inferred from such indications of worth, scrupulously the friend of Truth. His words were to this effect, "once, by instruction, I attempted to tamper with Colonel Pinckney, and touched with delicacy upon the possibility of a reconciliation with our government, hinting on the honours that would be his, should he openly declare his approbation of our measures. The result was indeed humiliating to me. I was instantaneously awed into silence, by the superiority of his patriotic virtue, and felt myself degraded by the office I had undertaken." Who that knew the purity of his affection for his country, could have suspected that sordid interest, or the highest honours, in the gift of the British Monarch, could have induced him to abandon his principles, and sacrifice her liberties.

> "There was not a purpose,
> Which his soul o'er formed, or hand acted
> But he could have bid the world look on,
> And what he dar'd to do, have dar'd to justify."—Rowe.

——— ♦ ———

GENERAL SIR WM. HOWE.

In my sketch of the celebrated festival at Philadelphia, "*the Mischeanza*," I have attempted a delineation of the conduct and character of this distinguished officer. The portrait which follows, I am inclined to believe, far more accurate, being drawn by one, who was a witness to all his actions, and who knew the bent of his disposition thoroughly. " Before he obtained the command of the Army, General Howe was regarded as an officer of high promise. Ambitious of military fame, he spared no pains to gain information, and to profit by their experience and improved talents, sought the society, and conversed only, with men of superior ability, and distinguished reputation. But, gratified ambition, soon altered his views, and induced him to pursue a course far less creditable, and even to have changed his nature. The sober, sedate soldier, degenerated into a licentious debauchee, and the society of the wise and virtuous abandoned for that of the most depraved and vicious youths, that could be collected, whose highest recommendations to favour, consisted in being able to excite a laugh, even by exposing to ridicule things the most sacred and worthy of admiration."

LORD RAWDON.

In looking over the papers of a very distinguished patriot, deceased, which had been put into my hands with the expectation of their affording me some information that would assist me in the completion of my second series of Revolutionary Anecdotes, I found it stated, that some short time previous to the attack upon the American Post on Sullivan's Island, a gold-laced cocked hat, had been picked up on the sea-shore, which had the name " *Rawdon*," distinctly printed within the crown. The writer makes his observations very fully on the folly of indulging inordinate ambition, and in the belief, that his Lordship had actually perished in a storm, that had a little before occasioned the loss of a very fine ship on the coast, proclaiming his fate as richly merited, for having quitted the free enjoyment of every blessing that rank and fortune could bestow, to bear arms against a people who had never injured nor offended him, and to whom it appears, that he had previously declared himself much attached. And upon what principle did

he do this! Not that he believed their resistance criminal, or
their resolution to defend their rights unnatural, or impolitic,
but solely " to seek the bubble reputation," and by aiming at
military distinction, to gain the smiles of his king, the favour
of an abandoned administration, and the aggrandizement of
fortune, and honours to his family. Happy had it been for
Carolina, had he perished before he trod on our soil, with hostile intention. Happy for his country too, as it would have
saved her reputation from much of that obloquy which has been
cast upon the British name; for, certainly there never was an
officer in command, who appeared so little scrupulous in devia-
ting wantonly from every principle of justice, nor one who,
with more rigid severity, followed the path of devastation and
bloodshed. Let a reference be made to the first series of Anecdotes of the Revolution, and sufficient evidence will be found,
of his uniform desire to oppress :—his despotic rule over the inhabitants of Camden, and its vicinity, while he commanded
there, and the ruthless barbarity with which multitudes were
daily led to the gallows. Let the wanton execution of Colonel
Hayne, be considered as the climax of his ambition, to put
down resistance by slaughter. Yet, other charges remain
against him that cannot be controverted or excused. On what
possible plea, I would ask, can his crafty insinuations against
Colonel Balfour be justified, on whom, when he found the current of popular opinion running strongly against this deed of
blood, he wished to throw the turpitude of the act, insinuating
in his famous letter to Colonel Lee, " that contrary to his inclination, and unceasing opposition, the nefarious deed had
been insisted upon, and finally perpetrated." Balfour was actually dead, or, (as the letter was written at sea, on his Lordship's passage to India,) not in a situation to defend himself, or
to rebut so unjustifiable a calumny, which renders the attempt
to injure, the more base and unpardonable. The fact is, Lord
Rawdon knew full well, that he had committed an act appalling
to humanity, which, at the moment, he took all possible pains
to justify, but, to which, when he found the opinions of society
decidedly opposed, he would have induced men to believe, that
he never had given a sanction. I will say nothing of *his*
14

amours, save only that it was an insult to the Army, and an
unjustifiable act of treachery to his king, to quit his command
when he knew that he was the only man in the country, equal
to the guidance of it—lured from his duty by the beauty and
fascinations of a lovely woman, to follow her to Europe.

> " Where were thy terrors Conscience—where thy Justice ?
> That this bad man should perpetrate such crimes,
> Insult thy sacred power, and glory in it."—FRANCIS.

PETER JOHNSTON, AND SOLDIERS OF THE LEGION.

Some weeks, spent in the Summer of 1826, under the hospitable roof of my early companion in arms, and justly valued friend, Judge Peter Johnston, of Abingdon, Virginia, gave considerable increase to my collection of Revolutionary Anecdotes, particularly such as related to the conduct generally, and gallant achievements of the officers and soldiers of the Legion. I shall, without hesitation, record many of them, more especially such as give evidence of the foresight, unruffled temper in the hour of peril, and intrepid conduct in action of my friend the Judge; persuaded, that they will be perused, with as much satisfaction, by my readers, as attended, when related, with delight to myself. I shall begin with a narrative of the *Murder* of Gillies, particularly as it happened under the eye of my friend, in the first rencounter which he ever had with the enemy.

GILLIES.

On the retreat of the army of General Greene into Virginia, subsequent to Morgan's victory at the Cowpens, a rencounter took place with the enemy, which strongly evinces the sanguinary disposition of Tarlton's dragoons, and the great superiority both in strength and courage of the Legionary Cavalry. The officers of the Legion were about seating themselves at the hospitable board of a friendly farmer, when Colonel Otho Williams, who commanded the Light Corps, rode up, attended by a countryman, mounted on a miserable tackey, and exclaimed, " to horse, gentlemen, the enemy are at hand." This honest fellow, seeing them pass his field, quitted his plough, and hastened to give us information of their approach. Captain Armstrong, with a small party, were immediately ordered forward to reconnoitre, and the countryman directed to serve him as a guide, but he decidedly refused to do so, unless a better horse was allowed him than that which he rode. Lieutenant Colonel Lee, wishing no delay, said to his Bugler, Gillies, a gallant youth, yet in early life, "change horses with him, Gillies, you, I am confident, do not fear to trust yourself on his tackey." The exchange was immediately made. Armstrong pushed forward, and Lee, with Lieut. Lewis, Peter Johnston, (then serving as a volunteer, and a candidate for a commission) with eighteen dragoons, with all expedition followed him. After riding a mile or more, Lee became impressed with the conviction that the countryman was in error, and determined to return to the farm house where dinner had been left, untouched, on the table. For this purpose he turned into the woods, through which the nearest course to the spot lay, and had gone but a short distance, however, from the road, when a report of pistols was heard, discharged by Armstrong's orders, to give notice that he had met the enemy. Lee immediately drew his men up in the wood by the road side. When Gillies was perceived urging his tackey to the utmost of his speed, striking him at every step with his cap, and smiling with the hope of enjoying the termination of the affair, not doubting but that relief was at hand. The moment that the British Dragoons arrived at a point opposite to the Legionary Detachment, the charge was ordered, but too late to save poor Gillies, who fell covered with wounds. Exasperated, almost to madness, to see an unarmed, beardless boy thus butchered while offering no resistance, the Legionary Cavalry rushed forward, and in a few minutes, fourteen of the British lay dead on the field. Their captain, and eight men, of whom several was severely wounded, made prisoners. The remainder of the party fled and escaped. Great prowess was exhibited in this unequal conflict by individuals. The British had thirty-seven dragoons engaged—the Americans but eighteen. Sergeant Power killed two men with his own hand, the last of whom died a martyr to his unbending, political prejudices, for, when assured that good quarters would be granted him on the surrender of his sword, he disdainfully replied, " it is far more grateful to me to die than to preserve my life, by yielding my sword to a rebel." Peter Johnston, the volunteer, must have fallen in the conflict, had not Sergeant Broom at the instant that a deadly blow was aimed at his head by a back-handed stroke of his sabre, sliced off a considerable part of the skull of the British dragoon who aimed it, and caused the uplifted weapon to fall without effect. The cry for revenge was universal, and Captain Miller, who commanded, would have been sacrificed, had it not been ascertained that the near approach of the main army of the enemy made it necessary immediately to retreat. The prisoners were, in consequence, sent to Colonel Williams, who sent them again forward to Head-Quarters. When the strong excitement of anger having subsided—the Captain was spared.

Interesting Sequel of the above Anecdote.

A strong and partial attachment to the country in which he had served, with distinguished reputation, and united with it an anxious desire to meet the early companions of his youth, several of whom still survived, having induced the Judge to visit the South. He left Richmond with that intent, in the winter of 1826, and had proceeded on his journey, as far as Guildford Court-house in North-Carolina, when an accidental overturn of his gig put a check to his progress. He had broken a shaft, and was not without a sufficiency of bruises, to make a temporary suspension of his journey desirable. A happy chance pointed out a wagon-maker's work-shop, immediately at hand, and, at a little distance, the house of Mr. Tatum, a gentleman of respectability, where he was assured he would meet with a kind and hospitable reception. It now occurred to Judge Johnston's recollection, that he could not be far removed from the spot in which he had first met the enemy, and witnessed the massacre of poor Gillies. To ascertain the fact, he related the adventure above stated to a company assembled around Mr. Tatum's fire-side, and speedily perceived by the expressive countenances of several of his auditors that the event was not unknown to them. When his narrative was concluded, a lady present feelingly exclaimed, " I have heard my

father relate the circumstances of that appalling tragedy, and
the death of Gillies, an hundred and a hundred times over,
and without the slightest difference from the statement you
have just made. He is within a short distance—I will summon him here. He will be delighted to converse with you,
and I am sure you will be glad to see him, particularly when I
tell you that he was the individual who had provided the dinner for yourself and brother officers, which the near and rapid
approach of the enemy compelled you to leave untouched. In
a little time, Mr. Bruce, the gentleman in question, arrived.
I will not attempt to state what the feelings of two genuine
patriots must have been, on meeting after a separation of forty-
two years, near the very spot where the one first engaged the
enemies of his country, and the other, at the conclusion of the
action, with his own hands, committed the body of the murdered Bugler to the grave. I can only judge of their sensations by the pleasure I feel in giving it publicity. Mr. Bruce
immediately offered to point out the spot where Gillies lay—
and renew the kind offers of hospitality which had, at first distinguished his feelings towards the officers Legion, and a refusal of them was only accepted, on the Judge's pleading ur-
gent business, which compelled him to go forward. When
about to depart, he asked, as usual, "what was to pay for the
shelter and entertainment afforded him." "Sir," said Mr.
Tatum, "a word on the subject would cruelly wound my feelings, your account with me was settled in the year 1781.
Your conduct was a receipt in full."

LIEUTENANT-COLONEL LEE.

THE conduct of Lee upon this, as well as every other occasion, was highly honourable to him. Envy, hatred and malice
have, on various occasions, assailed his character. Even personal courage has been denied him, but how is it possible to
think ill of a man, of whom that intelligent Soldier, General
Charles Lee said—"this gallant youth came a Soldier from his
mother's womb." Of whom General Greene said, in a letter,

dated February 18, 1782, " Lieut. Col. Lee retires, for a time, for the recovery of his health. I am more indebted to this officer, than to any other, for the advantages gained over the enemy in the operations of the last campaign, and should be wanting in gratitude, not to acknowledge the importance of his services, a detail of which is his best panegyric. " Who, in the memorable whiskey insurrection, was selected by General Washington to march into the interior of Pennsylvania, to put down, by his activity and decision, a revolt so disgraceful to America— and of whom Lord Cornwallis was known to say—" I am never at my ease when I know Lee to be in my neighbourhood, for he is prompt to discover the weak points in the position of my command, and certain to strike at them, when I am least prepared to repel his attacks. " I doubt if the calumnies which were levelled at his character ever reached him. Had they been communicated, I have not a doubt but that in the language of the Great Fabius, when reproached for avoiding a general engagement with Hannibal, he would have said—" I should be a coward, indeed, if I were to be terrified into a change of conduct by groundless clamours and reproaches. The man is unfit to be trusted, who can be influenced by the clamours or caprice of those he is appointed to command. "

—— ◆ ——

PETER JOHNSTON.

That implicit confidence should not be placed in the reports of deserters, has often been exemplified. Lieut. Col. Lee, in his Memoirs detailing the most interesting occurrences, which took place at the siege of Augusta, gives a striking example in point.* He states, that while rapid approaches were made by the besiegers against the British Post, commanded by Colonel Brown, an intelligent Sergeant of Artillery, who had pretended desertion expressly for the purpose of destroying the Maham Tower, likely from its commanding height to force a surrender, succeeded so far, by expressions of disgust, against the service

* Vide Lee's Memoirs, p. 106.

he had quitted, and the commander under whom he had served, as to lull suspicion, and to be actually placed in the situation the best calculated to effect it—*the Tower itself*. Lee, however, reflecting on the character of his adversary, of whom he had a very exalted opinion, and prepossessed in favour of his military talents, concluded that mischief was contemplated, and in that belief, removing the Sergeant from the Tower, committed him to the charge of the Quarter Guard. Subsequent information proved the prudence of his conduct. Colonel Brown, after the surrender of the Post, frankly declaring, that under the pretext of directing the fire of the besiegers against the Magazine of the Garrison, the Sergeant had engaged to use every art to gain admission into the Tower, and to destroy it. But, on the other hand, it has frequently happened that timely information received from deserters, of the intended movements of an enemy, has saved many a valuable life from destruction. I, with peculiar pleasure, mention one connected with the achievements of my friend, Peter Johnston, which happened at the same period, and at the same place, where, had not intelligence been communicated by a deserter of a contemplated attack on the trenches, Johnston and his entire command must have been cut off. The ditch of the besiegers was occupied by that officer, and twenty-four men. It was early in the night when a British soldier rushed into it, and said to Lieut. Johnston—"You know not, Sir, the danger which threatens you, a party of forty men, British soldiers and Indians, is now paraded, and ready to throw themselves on your command, and the labourers at the head of your entrenchment, and without immediate precaution, you will be cut to pieces." Information was instantaneously communicated to Captain Rudolph, who, with the Legion Infantry, was within a few hundred yards. Lieut. Johnston, at the same time, mounting his men on the reverse of the ditch, instructed them to remain, setting on their hams, until an order to rise should be given; when they were suddenly to gain their feet, and, with deliberate aim, fire on the approaching foe. In the interim he posted a centinel a little in advance, in a situation in which he could perceive the first movements of the enemy leaving their works towards him. The centinel soon brought intelligence that he had distinctly ascertained that the enemy were moving out of their fosse, which was not more than twenty yards from the head of the American entrenchment. Lieut. Johnston quickly heard, as a further evidence, the rattling of their cartouch boxes, and allowing them time to approach still nearer, gave the word to rise and fire. The effect was decisive. The British, instead of surprising, were themselves surprised. Contrary to expectation, they found their enemy prepared for their reception, and a very considerable portion of their force being cut off, the survivors fled with precipitation, and sought safety within their fortification.

Interesting interview between Lieut. JOHNSTON *and* MANNERING, *a Legionary Soldier.*

IN the Anecdotes of the Revolution, already published,* the singular interview which took place between Cooper of the Legion and myself, is particularly detailed. I have lately heard from my friend, Peter Johnston, of one which occurred between himself and a Legionary Soldier, which has equal title to be recorded. The Lieutenant, now Judge Johnston, was riding his circuit, and stopped at a stream to water his horses, where a wagoner had halted his team for a similar purpose. There was something in the man's countenance that reminded the Judge of a former acquaintance, and he said, " permit me, my friend, to ask if your name is not Mannering." " Yes, Sir, (replied the wagoner, it is.") " Did you ever serve, rejoined the Judge?" " I did, in the Legion commanded by Henry Lee, I was attached to the infantry of that corps." " Do you remember your Lieutenant, friend?" (continued the Judge.)— " What! little Peter Johnston; O full well do I remember him, the soldier's friend, as fine a white haired and spirited a youth as ever served." Then, "give me your hand, Mannering, and know that I am that very man." " You that man, replied the wagoner,—impossible,—Peter Johnston was a very likely youth,

* Page 152.

with light hair and fair skin, and you old gentleman are infirm
and weather-beaten, and over and above, grey as a badger."
A short conversation, however, set matters to rights. I will
not pretend to relate what the feelings of the parties were,
words would be inadequate to do justice to them. Suffice it to
say, that the Judge was delighted to learn that his former companion in arms had thriven in the world, and was, at the period
of their meeting returning home, having advantageously sold,
at Abingdon, the crop of the preceeding season.

Interview between Lieutenant JOHNSTON *and* DENNIS HAMPTON.

I SHALL now record another interview between my friend and
a soldier of the Legion, which is not without interest. Not
long after Congress had passed the act of March 18th, 1818,
granting pensions to the surviving soldiers of the Revolutionary
army, who were reduced to indigence, the Superior Court of
Law for Lee county, Virginia, was in session, when a man, who
appeared to be about sixty-two or sixty-three years of age, presented himself before the Judge, claiming the benefit of the
act. Judge Peter Johnston, who was on the Bench, was instantaneously struck with his countenance, and impressed with
the belief, that he had served under his command in the Legion
Infantry of Lee. To ascertain the fact, he therefore put the
following interrogatories. "Did you at any time serve in the
Continental army during the Revolutionary war?" "I was
in that service from the commencement to the close of the
war." "To what corps did you belong?" "To Lee's Legion."
"Were you with your regiment when it left the Northern and
joined the Southern army?" "I was." "Do you remember
any thing remarkable that occurred on the march at Petersburg?" "Nothing but that Colonel Lee ordered a man to be
hung there for an unpardonable offence." "Do you recollect
any particular circumstance that caused a great confusion at
Guildford Court-House." "I only remember that a Tory
was brought in a prisoner, about the time of our arrival there,
who was picketted and severely burnt in the feet and between

his toes to extort intelligence, and that no torture could induce him to speak." "What is your name." "William Hampton." "There was no man of that name attached to the Legion," said the Judge. "I have given my true name," said the soldier, "and did belong to the Legion." "Were you not wounded at Augusta, in Georgia, by a ball, which entered your foot at the instep, and passed out at the heel?" "I was, sir, but how came you to know that." "Let me first ask further, who commanded your platoon when you were wounded?" "Lieut. Peter Johnston." "Would you know your Lieutenant if you were now to see him?" "Certainly, sir." "Do you recollect to whom you sold a stout flea-bitten horse, on the day after possession was obtained of the British post." He stared intently in the Judge's face for a few seconds, when recollection breaking suddenly on his mind, he exclaimed, rushing forward and extending his hand with an expression of great cordiality, "I sold him to you, sir." "Answer me truly then," said the Judge, "is not your name, William Dennis?" "William Dennis Hampton is my name." "You certainly were Dennis, when with the Legion." "True, sir, but ever since my return to the neighbourhood in which I lived before the war, I have taken the name of Hampton." "How is that to be explained," said the Judge. "Very easily," replied the soldier, "my mother's name was Dennis, my father's, Hampton; they were never married, and I was known by my mother's name till her death, when I took the name of Hampton, in addition to that which I had previously borne." These multiplied interrogatories were put in order to discover the cause of the change of name, which being explained to the entire satisfaction of the Judge, it gave him particular pleasure to sign the certificate, which secured a pension to a veteran, who had ever been distinguished as an intrepid soldier, and zealous friend to his country.

JOSHUA DAVISON, OF LEE'S LEGION.

Joshua Davison, a private dragoon in the Legion, who had, on all occasions, behaved with distinguished gallantry, received

at the battle of Guildford, so severe a sabre wound, as to be
rendered unfit for immediate service. That every facility
might be afforded for his recovery, Colonel Lee gave him permission to quit the army, and retire to his father's house in
Prince Edward's county, Virginia ; and the more easily to accomplish his journey, allowed him to take his charger along with
him. The injury received, was in his right shoulder, which
totally incapacitated him from using his sword-arm. Before
his recovery was perfected, the invasion of Virginia was effected by Lord Cornwallis, and Tarleton, with his usual activity,
was scouring the country in every direction ; his particular aim
being to destroy the stores said to be deposited at Prince Edward's Court-House.

Davison hearing that a large body of British cavalry was
near the spot which he inhabited, resolved at once to take a
look at the enemy he had so often encountered ; and his sword-
arm being useless, loaded an old squirrel gun, and set out in
search of them. It accidentally happened, that passing through
a thick wood, he came upon a road, along which Tarleton had,
but a moment before, led his command. Determined to take
a nearer view, he at once fell into, and followed on their trail.
He had, however, advanced but a small distance, when he perceived a British dragoon, who had been plundering in the rear,
rapidly advancing, who drawing his sword, exclaimed, "surrender immediately, you rebel rascal, or you die." "Not so
fast, my good fellow," replied Davison, "I am not prepared to
yield ;" when raising his squirrel gun, with his left hand, he
fired it off, and laid his adversary dead at his feet ; seized his
horse and plunder, and carried them off in triumph. Some
years after, a gentleman asking him if he had been satisfied
by killing a single man ? "By no means," he replied ; "I re-
loaded my piece, and went in pursuit, but my firing had excited
such alarm, and Tarleton fled with such expedition, that I could
never have overtaken him, or I would have had *another shoot.*"

ROBERT HARVEY, OF THE LEGION.

ROBERT HARVEY, formerly a private dragoon in Lee's Legion, lately died at Fincastle. While actively engaged at Pyles' defeat, his horse was shot, and fell so suddenly and heavily upon him, that he found it impossible to extricate himself. A circumstance the more distressing, as a wounded Tory, who lay at a small distance, was using his utmost endeavour to take a decisive aim with his rifle, and dispatch him. His only chance for safety, rested on his remaining quiet under cover of his horse's body, till assistance could be afforded. At this moment, Captain Eggleston, with a few dragoons, passed by the wounded man, and perceiving one of them ready to thrust his sword through his body, forbade it, as an act of unnecessary cruelty. Harvey, observing that the Tory, unmindful of the favour shewn, (having a better aim at men elevated above him,) was about to fire, called aloud, "take care Captain Eggleston, or you are a dead man." The rifle was at the instant discharged, and the ball passed so near the Captain's ear, that it appeared to him that he had actually received a blow on the side of his head. Justly exasperated at the ingratitude of the wretch he had spared, Eggleston wheeled round, and by a thrust of his sword, dispatched him. Harvey was now relieved from the awkward position in which he lay, happy to escape not only the Tory, but the Catawba Indians, who were extremely active on this occasion, running over the ground for the sake of plunder, dispatching every wounded man, whether friend or foe. It gives me pleasure to state, that Harvey, at the conclusion of the war, by active industry, acquired a very handsome fortune, that he lived highly respected, and died regretted by all who knew him.

SERGEANT CUSACK, OF THE LEGION.

This important service was achieved before the Legion moved to the South ; but as the credit of it is due to a soldier of the regiment, I do not think that the recording of it in this place, will be deemed improper. While the British held possession of New-York, a gang of desperate marauders from that post, infested every part of the Jerseys. They were headed by Fenton, a robber of celebrity, whose activity destroyed every chance of travelling with security. To attempt his destruction, Sergeant Cusack, having six men under his orders, fitted up a wagon, in which such articles were exposed to view, as would, probably, allure to plunder, his associates being snugly concealed in its body. The stratagem proved successful: Fenton, and four of his associates, who incautiously rushed forward from a place of concealment, were fired on and left lifeless on the spot, while a reward of five hundred dollars, offered by the Governor of Jersey, was paid to the contrivers of it.

I have still another anecdote to relate, but of so melancholy a cast, as to be considered by some of my friends unfit for publication. That great severity was exercised towards a prisoner is true; and that it would have been unpardonable had the slightest trait of humanity been exercised by the individual, when he first burst into the apartment of the man, whose life he threatened to destroy, I am ready to grant. But the ferocity of his manner, gave just cause to apprehend that his object was to plunder, and his ultimate aim, death to the party assailed. It is difficult, at this late day, to form an idea of the savage mode in which the war was conducted, more especially between the native whigs and tories. I remember full well, to have heard a Lieutenant in the British 71st Regiment say, that a few days previous to the battle of Guildford, when Lord Cornwallis in vain endeavoured to trace the movements of General Greene, and to penetrate into his intentions, a young lad was brought into camp, who, when questioned with regard to the position of the American army, steadily replied, "you will find it soon enough." TARLETON, who stood by, being highly exasperated, drew his sabre, and making a chop at the youth's hand, deprived it of one of his fingers, saying, "Will you now tell me where is Greene." With steady and undaunted countenance, the reply was to the same purpose as before, "You will know time enough." Five times was the blow repeated, but with as little success. The youth had his secret, and he kept it. This cruelty was exercised by a Lieutenant Colonel of Dragoons, considered the pride of the army —its greatest ornament. "I wish," said Lord Cornwallis, (writing to him) "you could divide yourself into three parts— we can do nothing without you." Perhaps, the same spirit of decided attachment to the cause he supported, actuated him, and he was obstinately silent from the fear of answering questions, which might be put to him, improperly. At all events, the provocation was great, and examples of still greater barbarity were not wanting to palliate, if not to excuse the act. Immediately after the arrival of the Legion at Guildford Court-House, a countryman entered our quarters, (said my informant) having a prisoner in custody, and said to Colonel Lee, "While I was at table with my family, this fellow burst into the room, and putting the muzzle of his rifle to my breast, bid me deliver every thing that I had of value, or prepare to die. I knew that no sort of trust could be placed in this sort of gentry, and that the surrender of my property would be the signal for death. So I made a grab at his rifle, and turning it aside, it went off without doing me injury. A severe struggle followed, when getting entire possession of it, I struck him on the head with the but, and drove the cock-pin pretty deep into his skull. The severity of the wound made him my prisoner, and I brought him along for examination, for he seems a cunning chap, and I dare say, has plenty of intelligence, if he can be made to part with it." To all the questions put to him, not a word was returned in reply. The wounded man was obstinately silent. Dr. Irvine, Surgeon of the Legion, examining

the head, found that the skull was fractured, and that the brain
could be seen plainly through the hole made by the cock-pin.
Thrusting his finger into it, and drawing it back again, a portion of the brain remained on the point of it. "His obstinacy
must be overcome," was the universal cry. "Picket him,"
said Lee. The order was obeyed, but without effect. A red-
hot shovel was applied to the bottom of his feet, and even introduced between his toes, but not a feature of his countenance
was altered, nor did he utter a word of complaint. "The severity of his wound," said Dr. Irvine, "has produced insensibility—all feeling is destroyed—the man must die." "Place
him," said Colonel Lee, to Cornet George Carrington, "under
a corporal's guard, and be you answerable for him." The orders were obeyed. Night came on, and Carrington was quietly
reposing, when a musket was discharged, and a loud shout proclaimed that the prisoner had escaped. The fact was so—the
wounded man, who had been playing a part, no sooner perceived that a chance of escape was afforded, (the centinel
placed over him, becoming careless, from a conviction that one
so much injured, could not run) than he leaped up and ran off,
and though fired on and closely pursued, could not be overtaken.

PETER JOHNSTON was originally intended for the Church, his
father's great object was to make him an Episcopal Minister;
but he, himself, giving a preference to a military profession,
he clandestinely quitted the paternal mansion, and joined the
Legion as a volunteer, and candidate for a commission. I have
already said enough of him to prove, that he was a prudent,
active and most intrepid soldier. His diligence in acquiring a
knowledge of his profession was great—his attachment to literature, very conspicuous. Whenever there was the least respite
from duty, while his brother officers were seeking amusement,
or indulging in dissipation, Johnston would always be found at
his studies. The war concluded, he returned to his father's
house, and was well received. His thoughts were immediately
turned to law and politics. He acquired celebrity at the bar,

and was elected to the honourable station of Speaker of the House of Representatives. He did not, however, throw aside his youthful propensities, and actually figured as a General Officer at the head of the Virginia Militia; but being now more inclined to civil life, he accepted the appointment of Judge in some of the upper districts of the State, and now honoured, esteemed and admired by all who know him, resides, in the enjoyment of great comfort, at Abingdon, in Washington county. The Judge was early married to a lady of a most estimable character, and particularly distinguished by her talents and accomplishments. He has been the father of ten children, nine sons and one daughter, all of whom now live, with the exception of the eldest son, who has been dead for several years, leaving a disconsolate widow, who needs only to be seen to be admired and loved. I have often heard her declared, the very counterpart of her mother-in-law. The sons are all active, industrious and amiable men, and the daughter, a young lady of high promise.

CAPTAIN J. EGGLESTON.

I must apologize to my readers, and, in a particular manner to his family, for the incorrectness of my statement relative to the impatience which he displayed at the period that he lost his leg by amputation.* To my friend, Judge Johnston, I feel particularly indebted for the information that has made me sensible of my error, and enabled me to correct it. He assures me that after the decree of the attendant surgeons on the necessity of taking off the leg, that Major Eggleston submitted to the operation with the most exemplary composure and becoming fortitude, and that not the slightest sign of impatience was shewn by him from its commencement till it was completely finished.

I have erred too in another respect. I have attributed to him the capture of an entire foraging party of the British, on the

* Vide First Series, p. 125.

16

retreat of their army from Ninety-Six. Now I have no right to force upon him an honour that he never claimed. The act was Armstrong's, and Eggleston, with the frankness and generous feeling of a soldier, never failed to acknowledge it. Lee, knowing that the rich settlements south of Fridigs's Ferry, could alone supply the enemy with the forage which they would require, detached Eggleston, having Armstrong under his command, to the probable scene of action. An advantageous position was immediately taken, and their approach expected with anxious solicitude. A party of dragoons very speedily appeared, but from the mistiness of the day, their numbers could not be ascertained, and Eggleston immediately countermanded the order to charge, which had been given to Armstrong, till it could be satisfactorily discovered. Armstrong, however, who was one of the best and most intrepid soldiers that ever existed, either did not, or pretended not to hear the order of his commander, and dashed forward with irresistible impetuosity. Disarmed the leader of the British party, and so completely put them to route, that forty-five prisoners, together with all the foraging wagons, were taken without the loss of a single man. Congratulated on the importance of so brilliant an achievement, Eggleston, with great modesty, acknowledged that the credit of it was altogether due to his gallant companion, " for had my orders been obeyed," he said, " our triumph, in all probability, would not have been so perfect—a greater number of the enemy might have eluded pursuit and escaped."

CAPTAIN LINDSAY.

WITH this officer I never had the honor to form an acquaintance; he had quitted the service before I joined the Legion; but I have heard his military character very highly spoken of, and there is one instance of his intrepidity and skilful management, in imposing upon his enemy, that entitles him to particular commendation. To him, it was unquestionably owing, that Colonel Lee, and the detachment of the Legion which he commanded, escaped captivity, when surprised at the Spread

Eagle Tavern, near Philadelphia. Lindsay, while barricading the door of the Tavern, the more effectually to keep out the enemy, received a severe wound in the hand, which incapacitated him from the further use of his arms. Having nothing to do below, made his way to an upper apartment, and pretending to see the approach of friends from a neighbouring wood, set up a loud huzza, and beckoning with great eagerness, as if to accelerate their movements, so completely deceived the British, who imagined that a strong reinforcement was at hand, that they galloped off with precipitation, leaving Colonel Lee at liberty to quit the house, and retire at his leisure.

DR. MATTHEW IRVINE.

A SHORT sketch of the services of this meritorious officer, is given in my First Series, page 134. I am not satisfied with it. I have mentioned that his great fault, if fault it can be called, was the too constant exposure of his person in action, being frequently found in the heat of battle, when his post should have been in the rear, attending to the wounded. A departure, however, from the strict line of duty was productive on some occasions of great advantage. At Eutaw, for instance, Irvine could not avoid the temptation of taking a near view of the battle, and seeing General Greene alone, (his aids-de-camp being detached to different parts of the line with orders) he rode up, and assured him that he was ready to execute any commands that he might honour him with. "Quick then, (said Greene) to Colonel O. Williams, order him to bring forward his command with trailed arms, charge the enemy with the bayonet, and make the victory our own." The message was delivered with promptitude, and produced all the effect expected from it. Dr. Irvine married a lady at the conclusion of the war, distinguished for her patriotic attachment to her country, and settled, as a physician in Charleston. Let his medical friends speak more particularly of his professional celebrity. I shall be content to say, that for humanity to the poor, hospitality to strangers, warm and enthusiastic attachment to his friends, and perfect devotion to his family, no man has been more beloved and admired in society, than Dr. Irvine.

PARTICULAR ACCOUNT OF COLONEL BEAU-FORT'S DEFEAT.*

Col. Beaufort commanded a detachment of three hundred men, whom he had collected at Petersburg, in Virginia, and marched them to the South, that they might join their respective Regiments in garrison in Charleston. Arriving at Lenud's Ferry on the Santee, he received intelligence of the surrender of the City, and being at a loss what course to pursue, sent an express to General Huger, the Continental officer of the highest rank in Carolina, for instructions. An order was received to retire to Hillsborough, in North-Carolina, taking Camden in the route, in order to remove the ammunition and military stores deposited there, together with thirty or forty British prisoners, previously captured. If unable to remove the stores, his orders were to destroy them. Colonel Beanfort executed the order with precision. On his arrival at Camden, such stores as could not be removed were thrown into a neighbouring creek, and his route continued via the Waxaw settlement, towards Hillsborough. On the morning of the day on which the corps was attacked, Captain Adam Wallace, (Beaufort having resolved to halt for a day, in order to refresh his horses, which, from the heavy loads which they drew, were nearly exhausted,) invited Adjutant Bowyer to walk out with him. The latter observing that the spirits of his companion were unusually depressed, inquired the cause, and was answered, " I have known, for two or three days, that I am to die on this day." Bowyer laughed at what he deemed idle superstition ! Wallace became angry, and said, " You know full well, Sir, that I am not afraid of death. Whatever event may occur, I shall do my duty." The approach of a youth on horse-back, put an end to the conversation.—" Where from, my lad," exclaimed Bowyer. " I left Ridgeley's mills this morning," he replied, " and on my way hither, passed a large body of troops, most of whom were mounted—the rest well armed, and on foot."

* Communicated by Colonel H. Boyer of Fincastle, then acting as Adjutant to the Corps.

Wallace, turning quickly to Bowyer, asked " Do you not think my anticipations likely to be accomplished?" The lad was conducted to Colonel Beaufort, and, without the slightest deviation, repeated the information first communicated. The continuation of the retreat was instantaneously resumed, but the corps, had scarcely proceeded two miles, before the sound of Tarleton's bugles was heard, and a British officer was perceived riding forward, bearing a flag of truce. Adjutant Bowyer was instructed to meet him. Captain Kinloch, the advancing officer of the British, told Bowyer, that he could make no communication to him, and demanded a personal interview with Beaufort. A message to that effect being sent to the Colonel, he immediately repaired to the spot. Captain Kinloch then proposed, on the part of Tarleton, that Beaufort, and his detachment, should surrender as prisoners of war, on the same terms as those granted to the Garrison of Charleston, stating, at the same time, that his strength was upwards of six hundred men, half of them cavalry. The terms were, without hesitation, rejected by Beaufort, who did not believe that a force as strong could have reached the neighbourhood through which he was marching. Captain Kinloch assured him, on his honour, as a gentleman and officer, that his statement was correct; but, Beaufort, maintaining his opinion, dismissed the flag, returned to the ground where his detachment was drawn up, across the road, assembled his officers, and consulted with them on the subject of Tarleton's demand. The general opinion concurred with that of Beaufort. One officer, (Bowyer, thinks Captain Clayborne Lawson, of the 4th Virginia Regiment) proposed that the wagons should be brought together and a barrier to the enemy formed, behind which, the detachment should be posted. But, it was suggested that such a plan would probably further the views of the British commander, who might have sent forward only a small body of soldiers to amuse and detain Beaufort till a force adequate to his destruction could be brought up. Every arrangement was, in the interim, made for action. The British Cavalry quickly appeared, and commenced an attack, which was unsuccessfully continued for about fifteen minutes, when Major M'Arthur, who commanded

the Infantry, came up. The British force exceeded Beaufort's
detachment in number. Weakened by a variety of extra duty,
the command scarcely exceeded two hundred men. M'Arthur,
attacked the left with the bayonet, while the Cavalry assaulted
the right. The officers commanding platoons on Beaufort's
left, being all killed, and the command thrown into confusion,
Adjutant Bowyer was ordered to advance with a flag, and to
say to Tarleton, that he was willing to accept the terms offered
before the action began. The Adjutant remonstrated by saying, that as the firing still continued, the execution of the order
would be impracticable, exposing the bearer of the flag to the
shot of both parties. Beaufort repeated his orders, in positive
terms, and the Adjutant rode forward, with a handkerchief
displayed on the point of his sword. When close to the British commander, he delivered Beaufort's message, but a ball at
the moment striking the forehead of Tarleton's horse, he plunged
and both fell to the ground, the horse being uppermost. Extricated by his men from so perilous a position, the exasperated
Colonel rose from the ground, and ordered the soldiers to despatch him. They immediately gathered round, and several
cuts were made at him, which he had the good fortune to parry and avoid. By this time, Captain John Stokes and Lieut.
Willison, who occupied a position opposite to that where the
Adjutant was surrounded by the British Dragoons, and saw the
danger impending over him, directed their platoons to fire at
the group. They were well obeyed, and the bullets thrown
among the party around the Adjutant, frightening the horses,
gave him an opportunity of dashing through them, and effecting his escape unhurt. His horse was seriously wounded, but
not sufficiently so to prevent his carrying his master to a place
of security. The overwhelming force of the British then prevailed, and a dreadful massacre of the detachment followed.
The rage of the British soldiers, excited by the continued fire
of the Americans, while a negotiation was offered by flag, impelled them to acts of vengeance that knew no limits. Captain
Adam Wallace, too truly predicted his own death. He fought
with consummate intrepidity as long as he had strength to
raise his arm, and though quarter was tendered, refused to surrender.

SERGEANT MITCHELL.

THE intrepidity of this excellent soldier, merits particular notice. There were no Ensigns attached to the command, and when it was ascertained that a contest must ensue with Tarleton, the Adjutant selected Mitchell to bear the colours, as he had always been distinguished for correctness of conduct, and was connected with a family of high respectability. In the progress of the battle, Tarleton led an attack on the centre of the line where Mitchell was posted, with his Standard. The intrepid Sergeant was cut down, and the staff of his colours broken. Grasping the part to which the colours were attached, he retained it firmly in his hands, while dragged to a distance of fifteen yards. The British Dragoons now gathered round him, and would immediately have mangled him to death, but Captain Kinloch dismounted and protected him from their rage, declaring that so gallant a soldier, though an enemy, should not perish. Mitchell survived his wounds, though severe, removed at the close of the war to Georgia, became, from his acknowledged merits, a Brigadier General, and was, but a few years back, a hale and hearty man. This narrative of facts, comes within my own knowledge, except what I have said of Sergeant Mitchell, which I received from Judge Stokes.

      (Signed)   HENRY BOWYER.

A true copy attested.
    PETER JOHNSTON.

I WAS assured by General Thomas Pinckney, who visited the Hospitals at the Waxaws, in which the wounded were left, that he found many of them absolutely naked, having been stripped of their clothes, and that the average of wounds inflicted, amounted to sixteen to each man. This sanguinary massacre was one of Tarleton's most atrocious acts of barbarity, yet it exalted him in the favour of Lord Cornwallis, and raised his military reputation, in the opinions of the British nation, to the most exalted degree of perfection. That unnecessary severity was exercised, cannot be doubted. Five out of six of the American party, by the victor's official accounts, were either killed, or so badly wounded as to be incapable of being removed from the field; while *five* only of the British were killed and twelve wounded. I had always thought that this instance of deliberate barbarity was unparalleled, but a friend of mine,* who was actually a visitor at the Castle at Dublin, on the evening that a victory was announced, gained by Sir Charles Asgill, over the insurgents, assured me, that it was stated that twelve hundred men were slaughtered on one side, and but fourteen killed on the other. Curiosity, it was said, had led many of the peasantry to appear on the field, merely as lookers on, and from the desire to witness a battle, but the rage for slaughter, once began, the sword was used without too scrupulous an examination of principles, and all who came within its reach perished.

RALPH IZARD, SEN.

STRICT propriety required that I should have introduced the name of Mr. Izard, among the patriots, the most distinguished in the Civil Department, for there was not in the State, a man of more genuine and inflexible republican virtue, than himself. Had his disposition been more mild and conciliating, there can be no doubt, but that his usefulness would have been of far greater consequence, in promoting the cause of his country, but he knew not how to unbend; his general deportment was austere and forbidding, precluding the possibility of that free and confidential interchange of sentiment, essential to the perfection of political arrangements. His integrity was universally acknowledged; his firmness and devotion to the cause he had espoused, not to be shaken, and it would have been as impossible to have turned the sun from its course, as Mr. Izard from

* Mr. J. A. Smith.

what he conceived to be the path of honour. This steadiness of principle, made him less tolerant than he would otherwise have been, of the infirmities of others.

> " He knew not how to wink at human frailty,
> Or pardon weakness, that he never felt. "

He considered the honour of his country so closely connected with his own, that the slightest trespass against the one, was regarded as an insult to the other. On the election, which took place shortly after the evacuation of Charleston by the British, I had the honour of serving as a Representative from the same Parish with Mr. Izard, and particularly remember, on one occasion, an occurrence that will forcibly prove what I have asserted of his undeviating perseverance in the line of his duty. On some irregularity in debate, Mr. Izard, who had delivered his sentiments with more than ordinary warmth, was called to order by two members at the same instant. Mr. John Hunter, a sound man and true, was the one, the other an individual of fluctuating principles, who had more than once changed his political creed, adhering to the one or other side of the contending parties, as appeared the most congenial to his interests. He had once been in the Continental service. After the capture of Charleston, had changed his blue for a red coat, and continued with the British, till their blunders and uncontrolled severities, exciting the indignation of every individual, convinced him, that by the relinquishment of all that they had gained, they could alone escape the chastisement that awaited them, from the triumphant army of Greene. Removing into the interior country, and pre-eminently distinguished by his plausibility, in making, on all occasions, the worst appear the better cause, he effectually removed every speck of blame from his character, and was returned a Member to the Legislature. His course was now comparatively easy, and by dint of effrontery, and unlimited abuse of the friends he had lately quitted, if he did not persuade himself, at least persuaded others, that he was a perfect model of excellence, in every patriotic feeling. Calling loudly to order, he said, " Mr. Speaker, let me entreat, that you will compel the gentleman to confine himself to the

17

matter of debate. He is turning from his subject altogether."
Irritated by the interruption, and still more so by the ungracious mode in which the accusation was made, Mr. Izard, regarding him for some time with profound contempt, exclaimed,
"I am taxed, Mr. Speaker, by an individual, with turning from my subject; you, Sir, who know me well, and every member present, who does know me, will do me the justice to say, that inconsistency forms no part of my character. My accuser, may twist, and he may turn, without the risk of loss of character. He cannot know degradation." Then, turning, with a bow of profound respect to Mr. Hunter, he added, "You, Sir, are a gentleman, I will reply to you immediately."

When the motion for the establishment of County Courts throughout the State, was first made in the House of Representatives, Judge Pendleton, who was the mover, and most strenuous advocate, endeavouring to parry the severe sarcasms of Major Thomas Pinckney,* and others, said, rather tartly, "these gentlemen know not the inconveniences, to which the poor man is put, by being obliged to seek for justice at a distant Court, and at a great increase of expense, when, by the introduction of the system proposed, law will be brought to every man's door. Their riches makes the resource but of little importance to them. The poor feel it. The rich are beyond its reach." "Mr. Speaker," exclaimed Mr. Izard, with great agitation, both of voice and manner, "I am now able to solve a

---

* Judge Pendleton, among other arguments in favour of County Courts, said, "that they were admirably well calculated to promote sociability, and to strengthen the ties of friendship existing between gentlemen living in the same neighbourhood." "Mr. Speaker," said Major Pinckney, "there are few men better qualified to speak on this subject than myself. I have, as a recruiting officer, very frequently attended at County Court meetings, and invariably found them the best rendezvous for the enlistment of men. If gaming, drinking, cock-fighting, horse racing, biting, and gouging, are considered as likely to promote sociability and liberal feelings between neighbours, I agree with the gentleman in opinion, and will myself become the advocate of his favorite system. But my views of the subject are at present widely different, and with good reason; the cup of conviviality, it is true, was in constant circulation, but rarely with other effect than to produce strife and contention. The feuds of the parties were always advantageous to me. My comrades, in proportion to the quantity of liquor swallowed, grew more affectionately attached to me. I considered my brother lawyers as sure game. I invariably enlisted a considerable portion of the Bar, and had it not been for respect to the Bench, I conscientiously believe, that in many instances I could have prevailed on their Honours, the Justices, to have accepted of the bounty money also, and to have quitted the soft delights of inglorious ease, to engage in the shocks of battle, and all the dangers and turmoils of active service."

mystery, heretofore inexplicable. I have lately travelled in from the North, and to speak in military phrase, precisely in the trail of the Honorable Judge, the magnitude of his purchases have, I must confess, filled me with astonishment. Negroes in one section of the country, lands on speculation in another. Carringes in this city—draught horses, and agricultural implements in that. Blooded animals in all directions. And, why, let me ask, this inordinate desire to possess property? I will tell you, in the gentlemen's own words. He has ascertained that riches sets a man above law, and he is anxious to make the most of his own notable discovery."

As to the excellence of his understanding, and goodness of his heart, there were but few men of his day, that were considered as his superiors. Unbounded sacrifices had been made by him to support the cause of his country; his entire time and his talents were devoted to the performance of the duties which the high stations to which he was called, required of him; yet prejudices, arising, as I have stated, from his distant behaviour to all who were not his immediate friends and associates, in mixed society, caused insurmountable prejudices to exist against him. I have one strong proof in point. General Barnwell, who was an enthusiastic admirer of Mr. Izard, knowing that he would, at any time, make a libation of his blood to serve his country, endeavoured to obtain the consent of Colonel Wadsworth of the interior, on most subjects a man of unbounded liberality, to join him in the endeavour to make Mr. Izard the Governor of the State, at the moment when French aggressions gave strong indication of a determination to disturb the peace and tranquillity of the Union. "Barnwell, (said the Colonel) I would willingly promote your wishes on any other point, but with regard to Mr. Izard, my mind has long been made up. He may, perhaps, in an hour of humility, acknowledge the superiority of the Almighty, but I am persuaded, that over all created beings, he believes that he has such decided superiority in every respect, that he believes that all who look on him, view him with reverential awe, and that in every point there is an obligation to yield the most perfect submission to all that he is pleased to deem right and proper to be done. For such a man I can never vote."

Particulars relative to the Death of Mr. John Inglis, *killed by an unfortunate mistake, at a Plantation, near Charleston, in the year* 1781.

The following extract from a series of letters, published in the New-York Statesman, was sent to me from Philadelphia, by my friend Dr. Mease, with a request that I would inquire into the particular circumstances of the case, and forward them to him, that they might be transmitted to friends in Scotland, who (though strongly prepossessed in favour of the American character and conduct of our citizens, during the struggle to obtain the independence of their country) declared themselves cruelly mortified by the representation of a murder, distinguished by wanton and unparalleled barbarity.

EXTRACT.

" A tablet on the wall, opposite my seat, very forcibly attracted my attention, and did not bespeak a very liberal spirit in the citizens of Inverness, towards the Americans. It was erected in memory of Mr. Inglis, sometime merchant at Savannah, Georgia. The inscription states, 'that he was murdered by a band of ruffians, hired by the execrable Congress, on account of his fidelity to his king and country, while living with a friend, near Charleston, South-Carolina.'"—*Carter's Travels.*

In my first publication of Revolutionary Anecdotes, (p. 251) the death of Mr. Inglis is mentioned, with the strongest expressions of sincere regret. Called upon as I have been, for particulars relating to it, I shall now give a full statement of facts, as they occurred, declaring a thorough conviction in my own mind of their perfect authenticity. I was intimately acquainted with Mr. Inglis in Europe, and knew him to be, in his political opinions, a man of the greatest liberality, adhering to the cause of Britain, but without any harsh or illiberal prejudice against America. He arrived in Charleston, in the year

1780, seeking to improve his fortune as a mercantile adventurer, but meeting with no immediate success, was induced by his friend and relative, Dr. Cletheral, to accompany him on a visit to his plantation, on the Horse-Shoe, about forty miles distant from the city. Colonel Harding, and a few of his followers, who, about that period, had raised the standard of opposition against the tyranny exercised universally throughout the country, by the British army, were in the neighbourhood in close concealment, and Dr. Cletheral being considered an obnoxious character, an immediate determination was formed to secure him. His house was accordingly surrounded, and entered with so little noise, that Mr. Robert Read, of Prince William's, who was one of the party, assured me that he roused Dr. Cletheral out of a sound sleep, before he knew that he had any danger to apprehend from an enemy. Mr. Inglis hearing a noise in his friend's chamber, quitted his bed, and ran into an entry that separated their apartments, when being called upon to declare his name, no sooner replied *Inglis*, than the contents of a rifle were poured into his breast—he fell, and expired without a struggle. Greatly agitated by so unlooked for an event, Dr. Cletheral feelingly exclaimed, " You have done a deed, gentlemen, which must cause your deepest regrets— Mr. Inglis is a perfect stranger in your country, who never cherished a thought or sentiment injurious to America." " How can you make that assertion, (exclaimed the man who had done the deed) and utter in our presence so gross a falsehood ; for a month has not elapsed, since Colonel Thomas Inglis had me haltered for a very trifling offence, and would have hung me, but for the interposition of an officer of the Regulars, whose humanity saved my life." " But (rejoined Dr. Cletheral,) the unfortunate victim of your wrath, is not Col. Thomas Inglis, but Mr. John Inglis, a native of Inverness, lately arrived from Europe, who never, in a single instance, bore arms against America." " Then, indeed, (said the man, whose name was Fraser,) I bitterly lament my precipitation ; for I also am from Inverness, and knew John Inglis intimately well. We were school-fellows, and in our boyish days, play-fellows and friends. The intimacy, Doctor, subsisting between yourself and Colonel

Thomas Inglis, caused the mistake—for hearing the name of your companion, I concluded that he must have been the man by whom I had been so cruelly outraged a little before, and I considered the thirst for vengeance justifiable both in the eyes of God and man." The facts, as I have related them, I had from Mr. Read, who was present, and, at an after period, from the family of Mr. Inglis himself, with whom I lived on so intimate a footing, as to have accompanied Mr. Alexander Inglis, brother to the deceased, to the field, where, in conjunction with Captain David Campbell, of the British sixty-third regiment, I had the good fortune to accommodate differences, and bring about a perfect reconciliation between the parties, who had been previously, intimate friends.

To place a tablet then, on the wall of a Church so incorrect in every particular, appears to trifle with truth, and wilfully to lie in the face of Heaven. It must necessarily too, keep alive prejudices that should long ago, have been buried in oblivion. I would appeal to the daughters of Mr. Alexander Inglis, now settled in Inverness, who must remember me well, and to Mr. John Deas Thompson, a respectable gentleman, attached to the Navy-Office of Great Britain, if they do not know me incapable of making a false statement relative to the unfortunate occurrence which took place, and even if they themselves, have not constantly heard it related, exactly as detailed by me.

——— · —

Howe's Narrative, relative to an American Officer.

In the year 1785, I received the Anecdote which follows, from General Robert Howe, of North-Carolina, then a resident in New-York:—

"I was walking some months since, in one of the principal streets of this city, when my attention was attracted by the remarkably handsome figure of a man, who, with a frantic wildness in his eyes, and a countenance filled with horror, betrayed the most unequivocal symptoms of distraction. The phrenzy of passion seemed occasionally to subside, but the traces of a deep and settled melancholy that remained, left no doubt with regard to the anguish that preyed upon his heart. His body was wasted to a skeleton, his complexion of a deadly paleness. His coat, that had once been regimental, was thread-bare, and plainly indicated the poverty and wretchedness of the wearer. Approaching nearer to him, I, with grief and aston-ishment, recognized the features of Major——, a youth of pre-eminently polite and amiable manners, and of distinguished bravery. At the same moment he perceived me, and noting the fixed attention with which I viewed him, attempted, with hurried steps, to avoid an interview, and retire. My heart beat high with pity and affection : I rushed towards him, and ere he had retreated many paces, held him firmly in my arms. Finding it impossible to avoid conversation, he strove to assume an air of cheerfulness and composure, and by every possible means, to turn my attention from the object in which my whole heart was interested, to wit, to discover the cause of the anguish which preyed upon him. 'Come, come, my brother soldier,' I said, 'let no foolish pride, no unwarrantable delicacy, tempt you to conceal your sorrows from a friend who loves you—I have secretly witnessed the tumults of your mind—an agitation bordering on despair—and am resolved never to quit you, till you communicate the cause of your grief, and put it in my power to restore your mind to its wonted tranquility.' While yet I spoke, a boy, who had been sent to the Post Office, pre-sented a letter, and retired. The Major received it with trembling hand, anxiously broke the seal, and with precipitation run-ning his eyes over the contents, exclaimed in ecstasy—'My God, my God, I thank thee! Your goodness alone has saved me from impending destruction—from the mad suggestions of my own wicked heart. How, my dear General, shall I presume to look upon you, when I confess, that though a soldier, I have shrunk from the frowns of adverse fortune, and feeling my-self unequal to the trial of combatting the miseries of poverty, had resolved, by my own sinful deed, to terminate existence. My pistols are loaded—they now lie on my desk, and the hand which till now, has never been employed, but in the field of

glory and honour, would, within an hour, have been lifted
against my own life.   You are no stranger to the zeal with
which I have served my country : but, probably, know not, that
to support appearances, my fortune has been sacrificed—my
youth having been spent in the exercise of arms, my patrimony
has been dissipated.   Creditors, whose hearts knew no compas-
sion, have driven me to destruction.   To die, seemed the only
means by which I could escape the miseries of abject penury,
and the horrors of a jail.   A beneficent Providence has saved
me from the crime of self-destruction.   By the letter which
you saw me receive, I am informed of the death of a relation,
who has unexpectedly left me a very considerable estate.   My
debts shall be paid, and through a life, which I shall endeavour
to make useful to my country, next to my God, I shall return
thanks to you, to whose compassionate attention it is owing that
I now exist.' "

Another Narrative, respecting an unfortunate Officer.

I INTRODUCE this Anecdote, with a view to caution my young
countrymen not to place too great a reliance on their ability to
guard against, and repel the encroachments of vicious propensities.   I cannot doubt, but that the individual, concerning whom
I am about to speak, was in the early career of life, in his own
opinion, strong in virtue, and in his adhesion to just and dignified principles, firm as adamant ; yet, in an unlucky hour, his
mind, impelled by the indulgence of heedless dissipation, his
strength abandoned him, and he fell, never to rise again.   I
would, on no consideration, mention names.   I will not even par-
ticularize the State to which he belonged.   For worlds, I would
not lacerate the feelings of surviving relatives, if such there
be—who would know that the statement, though heart-rending
in the extreme, is by no means exaggerated.   *Horatio*, for so I
shall take the liberty to designate him, was born to fortune—
his estate afforded him more than an ample competency to supply all his wants ; he could give indulgence also to every rea-
sonable desire.   He entered the service at an early period of

the Revolution, and by his zeal and activity, acquired both rank and reputation. Promotion gave an opportunity to gain additional laurels, and he did not fail to improve it. His character as an officer, stood high in the army; and there were few names more formidable to the enemy, or more highly respected than that which he bore. Uncommonly handsome in person, and engaging in manners, there was a strong prepossession in his favour wheresoever he appeared. Liberal as well as brave, that sentiment was uniformly cherished and improved. Few men have ever enjoyed a greater share of favouritism than himself. The superiority of his personal attractions were, indeed, such, that it was often said, that a better model would never be found to afford a just representation of the God of War. His attachment to company proved his ruin. His income was not equal to the payment of his expenses—he became involved, and contracted heavy debts; to the payment of which being altogether incompetent, he lost all respectability of character, and rapidly depreciated, till sunk into the most abject state of wretchedness and depravity. When once the strict line of propriety is abandoned, there is no saying to what degradation the mind will not submit. Departure from duty is palliated and excused, and enormities justified, that would previously have been regarded with horror and detestation. He who was accustomed to give with liberality—whose purse was always open, while his friends stood in need of succour and assistance, became now so eager to raise funds to support his extravagances, so little sensible of shame, so incessantly pressing in his demands on the generosity of all who were inclined to aid him, that he was considered a scourge to society, so decidedly obnoxious, that his friends and associates were compelled to withhold assistance, and leave him to his fate. Dissipation had regularly kept pace with the increase of pecuniary distresses. He drank to excess, and with the meanest wretches in society. Application for aid was next made to strangers and loungers about the taverns, and every pot-house, in the city he inhabited. This resource for a time afforded relief, it lasted only for a short period. It was not even then, that the climax of his miseries had arrived. Among other talents possessed,

18

he was an excellent musician, and was a perfect master of the violin. A talent, which had been once a source of pleasure and amusement, was now exercised to gain bread. But bad habits, strengthened by indulgence, had become so powerful and inveterate, that his services were engaged, even at fandangoes and negro weddings; and where money could not be obtained, he was content to stipulate for a sufficiency of food, and the liberty of calling for liquor *ad libitum*.

Spirit of ENTERPRIZE, *a distinguished characteristic of the* AMERICAN TROOPS.

COLONEL WHITE, OF THE GEORGIA LINE.

WHILE the siege of Savannah was carrying on, an enterprize was effected by Colonel White, of the Georgia Line, which has more the air of a romance, than of a reality, though unquestionably accurately stated by Dr. Ramsay, in his History of the Revolution, in South-Carolina.* Captain French, of the British army, had taken post with one hundred and eleven men, near the river Ogeechee. There were, at the same place, five vessels, manned with forty sailors, and carrying from four to fourteen guns each. The whole surrendered to Colonel White, Captain Elholm, and three others. It may well be supposed that stratagem was employed by the victorious party. Colonel White, by keeping up a number of fires, judiciously placed around, impressed on the enemy the belief that he was completely surrounded, and that an immediate surrender would alone save his men, from being cut to pieces. On a peremptory call for submission, Captain French agreed to lay down his arms. The vessels were burned, and the whole command being cautiously deprived of the means of defence, were marched into camp at Sunbury, by the proud and happy conquerors.

ACTION AT KING'S MOUNTAIN.

THE Post at King's Mountain was commanded by Colonel Ferguson, one of the most intelligent and intrepid officers of the British army, and I may safely add, one of the most dangerous enemies to America, from the influence he had acquired

* Vol. II. pp. 42, 43.

over the tory inhabitants of the upper Districts, and his indefatigable zeal in training them to arms and strengthening their
attachments to the Royal interests. He had at his post, upwards of one hundred Regulars, and a thousand men of his
new levies. In opposition to him, several parties of volunteers,
under their respective leaders, Cleaveland, Campbell, Shelby,
Savier and Williams, from the mountains, Lacy and Hill, from
the surrounding country, approached with decided hostility.
Superiority of command was not claimed by any individual.
Guided by their resentments, and determined to check the encroachments of a merciless foe, the post was assailed at three
different points, but in repeated instances without the least effect. The several attacking columns were beaten back with
loss. The resolution to conquer, was not, however, to be subdued. The charge was again and again renewed, when Colonel Ferguson falling, by a well-directed rifle shot, the tories
became panic-struck; called aloud for mercy, and without further opposition, surrendered. It may be truly said, that hardy
enterprize, supported by irresistible courage, produced this momentous achievement, important in its consequences beyond
calculation: for, had victory crowned the efforts of Ferguson,
to repel his enemy, not only vigour would have been added to
the exertions of the tories, who had decidedly favoured the
Royal cause, but the wavering might have been induced to side
with the triumphant party, and enabled Colonel Ferguson, to
accomplish the great object of his ambition, to depress the
American people by the exertions of their own degraded and
perfidious brethren. It would have afforded an excellent opportunity for two such distinguished tories as Cunningham and
Fletchall, to have united their forces to his victorious command, who had previously, from the confession of one of their
most intimate associates to Dr. Read, kept aloof till it should
be ascertained which army was most likely to gain an ascend-
ancy over the other, *when they could*, with safety, make a
choice of sides.

COLONEL MEIGS.

The expedition of this meritorious officer against the British post at Sagg's-harbour, Long Island, richly deserves to be recorded. Colonel Meigs had served with distinguished reputation in Canada, and was present at the assault of the lines at Quebec. In the orders of General Wayne, on the reduction of Stoney Point, we find him highly complimented, and thanked, for the gallant manner in which he led his Regiment to the attack. But, the celerity of his movements—the clear perceptions of his judgment, in arranging his plans, and carrying them successfully into effect, in the attack of the foe at Sagg's-harbour, was the event in his military career, which, in the highest degree, exalted his reputation.

Ordered by General Parsons, who had received intelligence that the enemy were making large collections of grain, forage and horses, on the East end of Long Island, to impede their operations and attack their posts, he embarked with his command in thirteen whale-boats, and pressing rapidly forward, partly by land, and partly by water, with one hundred and thirty men of his detachment, arrived at Sagg's-harbour, attacked the enemy with fixed bayonets, and though greatly annoyed by the fire of a sloop of twelve guns, and seventy men, burnt twelve brigs and sloops, five hundred and twenty tons of pressed hay, oats, corn, and other forage, in considerable quantity, ten hogsheads of rum, and a large store of merchandize, and carried off ninety prisoners, soldiers and sailors, having, in twenty-five hours, transported his detachment ninety miles, without the loss of a single man, killed or wounded.

COLONEL BARTON.

I am sensible that I am about to repeat a thrice-told tale, but there is so much the appearance of romantic gallantry in

the exploit of Colonel Barton, that I trust I shall be pardoned
for making still another effort, to keep it in view of all who delight to give to patriotic enterprize the applause which is its
due. Sometime in July, 1777, Lieutenant Colonel Barton,
having received information that Major General Prescott, who
commanded the British and foreign troops, on Rhode Island,
had established his Head-Quarters at a country house, at some
distance from the main body of his army, resolved on the attempt to bring him off as his prisoner. To accomplish his purpose, thirty-eight men were selected from the line, who, being
embarked in five boats, set out on the expedition. The task
which they had to perform was difficult and dangerous. The
British posts on the Island, were many and strong, and reported to be ever on the alert ; while a considerable Naval arma-
ment protected it on every side from invasion. The ships and
guard-boats being passed in the dead of night with muffled
oars, and no discovery made, Lieut. Colonel Barton landed his
party, and having first secured the sentinel, entered the General's apartment, and took him from his bed. His Aid-de-camp
made a desperate attempt to escape by leaping from a window,
but was pursued and speedily secured also. Expedition was
now necessary and essential to safety. A large body of Dragoons lay in the neighbourhood, and signal rockets, thrown into
the air from different quarters, showed that a general alarm
had already spread. Every comfort was afforded the prisoners, that circumstances would allow, and Lieut. Colonel Barton
had, at early dawn, the good fortune to land them in safety,
after a passage of ten miles, at the spot within the American
lines, from which he had set out. I remember many years
since to have heard a highly respectable clergyman say, that in
the year 1746, he resided on the Post-road between Colodden
and Aberdeen, and that in the evening of the day on which the
battle was fought, on which the fate of the Empire depended,
that he had received into his house an English officer, from the
South, hastening to join the Duke of Cumberland's army.
During the night, the Aid-de-camp carrying the news of victory to London, demanded hospitality also, and fully relating
the extent of the triumph over the forces of the Pretender,

the Englishman exclaimed " would to Heaven that I had that formidable rebel, *Gordon of Glenbucket*, as my prisoner, I would fasten him up in a cage, and carry him as a show through England, where his terrific name has made such an impression, that there is not a clown throughout the country, who does not believe that he eats at least one child every morning for his breakfast. I should speedily make a most ample fortune." I was present when a particular friend of my own, sometime after Colonel Barton's successful expedition, addressing him with a very serious air, said, " I wish, my dear Barton, that I had you caged, that I might show you as the hero, who had made a prisoner of the renowned and formidable British General Prescott. I would ask no better income, than the cash that would be received from the exhibition." The Colonel appeared delighted at the thought, and I seriously believe, that if a cage had been in preparation, he would cheerfully have stepped into it, for the pleasure of enjoying the wonder and astonishment that would have been displayed, when the gaping spectators discovered that he was *but a man.*

There was one trait in the American character, which every man of candour must admit, has not been rewarded with the commendation to which it was richly entitled. I allude to the spirit of enterprize, which, in so many instances caused the bold defenders of their country, to submit to every species of privation without murmuring, and to brave all danger at the call of duty. If we regard them collectively, I deem it impossible that the evils of disease and famine, together with the absolute want of decent clothing, could have been sustained with more perfect resignation, than that which, under the most appalling trials, marked the general conduct of the Southern army, under the Generals, Gates and Greene.* Nor do I view

* This exhibition of patient suffering, was what Captain Barry, of the British Army, generally distinguished by the name of "Harry Barry Secretary," was pleased to style *passive courage.* Loth to allow any species of merit to the Americans, he was wont to say. "your soldiers know how to suffer, but they are destitute of that activity and energy that distinguishes Britons, who delight to encounter difficulty and seek danger, and who are never so happy as when an opportunity offers of displaying intrepid daring." But where, I wonder, was his energy—where the bold, daring of the Briton, when at Eutaw he surrendered his sword to Lieut. Manning, presenting the handle of his dirk in an imposing attitude, and threatening to shoot him if he offered resistance. It must, like the courage

with less admiration, the steady perseverance of that intrepid band of Northern Heroes, who surmounted all the difficulties of the wilderness, when marching against Quebec. The hardships encountered by the first, are fully detailed in my first series of Anecdotes. I will briefly notice those of the last.* For the distance of three hundred miles, not a house was seen, nor a human countenance to cheer; not a friend to direct them in their course. Incessant labour and fatigue destroyed their strength and damped their energies. They were either compelled to drag their batteaus up rapid rivers, or to transport them on their shoulders over difficult carrying places; woods almost impenetrable, deep morasses, and precipitous mountains perpetually impeded their progress. Disease was rapidly thinning their ranks, and famine, in its most ghastly form, threatened their entire annihilation. Already their dogs, their cartouch-boxes, and shoes, had been greedily devoured, and when the last pittance of food was distributed, a distance of thirty miles was to be traversed, before it would be possible to obtain any further supply. The stoutest hearts might have been appalled; the most determined courage been subdued. A Colonel Enos, and one-third of the detachment shrunk from their duty and returned; the rest, supported by their enthusiastic attachment to their country, with unabated fortitude and constancy, persisted till the gratifying appearance of the habitations of men assured them that the severest of their trials had ended. Received with kindness by the Canadian inhabitants of the frontier settlements, the spirit of enterprize regained its pristine vigour, and although from the firmness of Carleton, and indefatigable exertions of M'Lean, these bold adventurers reaped not the reward of their labours, yet, it must be allowed, that they deserved it.

of *Acres*, in the Play, have oozed out at his fingers' ends, for he yielded his weapon without opposition, and was led off the field by a man of rather diminutive size, although he reported himself " *overpowered and taken by an immense Virginian.*"

* I am very ready to acknowledge, that this is a narrative that has often met the public eye; one wherein I can introduce nothing of novelty, nor add any incident strikingly interesting, but it is so admirably calculated to prove, when actuated by the love of freedom, and supported in their exertions by devoted attachment to their country, what privations men can patiently submit to—what dangers encounter—what difficulties overcome, that I shall meet with pardon, for giving it a place in my present series.

IMPOSITIONS OF FOREIGNERS EMPLOYED BY THE UNITED STATES.

I AM sensible that in the opinion of many European politicians, the popular leaders, throughout the American continent, contemplated, from the earliest dawn of the Revolutionary contest, the dismemberment of the empire, and total separation of their country from the dominion of Great Britain. Yet, I am far more inclined to believe, that their views did not extend beyond the immediate redress of existing grievances, and the obtaining from the King and Parliament a satisfactory pledge against any further encroachments on their rights and liberties. Had the wish to establish the independency of the Colonies existed, it cannot be doubted but that greater pains would have been taken to secure its accomplishment, and some traits of a regular system been discovered, of a combination of influential and aspiring men, devoting their time and their talents to that object. It proceeds not from the indulgence of national vanity that I say, that there was certainly no deficiency of foresight, or of political intelligence exhibited by those bold and adventurous spirits, who first stepped forward as the advocates of liberty, or want of zeal in encouraging the resistance they had dared to recommend. But the sinews of war were wanting. The munitions necessary for defence, in no degree proportionate to the quantity required, and although opposition to hostility was by general consent determined on, its successful issue, even to the most sanguine, was considered extremely problematical. The deficiency of military stores being confessed, (and it certainly does not appear an imaginary want) the chance of obtaining them was rendered extremely precarious, and, from the vigilance of the enemy's cruizers, almost impracticable. But had they abounded, the want of men, properly trained to arms, and of officers competent to command

19

them, would, necessarily, have paralyzed exertion; and to men of less sanguine temperament, obscured with deeper shades the gloomy prospect before them. It is presumable, also, that with the view to get rid of the arbitrary dictates of a foreign authority, that individuals aspiring to the attainment of honour and renown, would, unceasingly, have endeavoured to qualify themselves to meet on equal terms, the experienced enemy with whom they had to contend. But this was far from being the case; and it was not till the sword was actually drawn, that the studies were commenced, and the information sought for, which ought to have been previously perfected. From this source, many disasters which attended the early efforts of the American arms is to be attributed. Anxious to obtain knowledge in military tactics, and to qualify themselves for service, they indulged a credulity that nothing but the ardour of their zeal could excuse. They believed every foreigner who called himself a soldier, to be one in reality, and every pretender to rank, a gentleman. Deception was too often practised with success. Individuals were engaged as engineers who were ignorant even of the most simple axioms in mathematics; and Counts and Barons received into the best society, and caressed as devoted admirers of the cause of liberty, who had never in their own country known other service than that of administering to the wants and caprices of their superiors, or sought employment with any other views, than the aggrandizement of their own fortunes and consequence. The genuine frankness and hospitality of Carolinians made them peculiarly the dupes of impostors. All who promised largely were considered as competent to the performance of their promises, and confidence was invariably found the concomitant of profession. The history of the war in the interior of our own State, affords ample proof of the incapacity of the engineer directing the operations at the siege of a fortress of importance to perform the duty assigned to him. From his want of judgment, approaches were made at the very point where the enemy were least vulnerable, and a repulse, attended with the loss of many valuable lives, the immediate consequence. The sieges of all the other British posts, directed by Marion, Sumter and Pick-

ens, and in an especial manner, by Lee and Maham, were speedily brought to a successful termination. That of Ninety-Six alone proved unfortunate.

Of the impositions practised on the credulous, with regard to the assumption of rank and title, they too frequently occurred to excite surprise. I have, in very many instances, seen men familiarly associating with, and seated at the tables of distinguished characters, who, had they occupied their proper stations, would have been placed in attendance behind them. I will, in evidence, bring forward one instance, well remembered by many persons now living. An individual, calling himself the Baron de Glaubuck, was greatly caressed, and freely received in many of the most respectable families in Charleston. I never could perceive a single trait of excellence about him: his great delight was to make a mockery of the religion he professed, and to endeavour to amuse those who would listen to him with the prowess he had displayed in cutting to pieces unfortunate tories who were persuaded, by his pretending to coincide in opinion with him, to declare their sentiments in favour of the Royal Government. In the field, as might well be supposed, he was far more active in pursuit, when victorious, than in opposing an enemy who resisted. Repeated acts of fraud drove him ultimately from society, when it appeared that his origin was as humble as his pretensions to distinction had been extravagant. I was myself informed by a Pennsylvania soldier, who had been his early friend and comrade, that he had made his first appearance in America as a Yager, and had deserted his colours, far more from the hope of bettering his fortune, than any attachment to the cause or to the country, of which he professed himself an enthusiastic admirer.

That the highest advantages were derived to America, from the ardent zeal and daring enterprize of many distinguished foreigners, no one can, or would wish to deny. The services rendered by General Lafayette, by Baron Stenben, Pulaski, De Kalb, Ternant, Fleury, Duportail, Cambrey, Lemoy, Gouvion, demand our warmest applause, and very many others while they covered themselves with the palm of renown, excited in the bosoms of the people of America a corresponding tribute of affection and gratitude, that will, to the end of time, cause them to be classed among the most distinguished of the heroes, whose firmness and intrepidity established in our country, the blessings of Liberty and Independence.

There were many others entitled to high encomiums. One instance, in which modest merit ventured not to claim the distinction which was its due, I take a pleasure to record, and am not without hope that it will be received with approbation.

A gentleman, of prepossessing appearance, a subject of Russia, genteel in manners and highly gifted in accomplishment, appeared in the cantonments of the army, soliciting, though fruitlessly, a continental commission. The evil that I have mentioned above began to be severely felt; and confidence, too often bestowed improperly, gave place to a suspicion, that in many instances appeared inconsistent with propriety. The commander-in-chief complained to Congress that he was wearied out by foreigners perpetually demanding employment when he had little to bestow, and his mind far from being satisfied with the qualifications of the applicants. The uniform good conduct and genteel deportment of the individual in question gained for him the general esteem of the army, and particularly attracted the attention of General Irvine, who received him into his family, and appointed him his aid-de-camp. The general opinion was, that he was as certainly a man of rank, as he was acknowledged to be of high endowment and finished education ; but on that head he preserved the most profound silence. Assuming the name of Rose, he would have passed himself off as a physician, but it was speedily discovered that he possessed but a very slight knowledge of the medical art, acquired during a short residence with Dr. Wisendolf, at Baltimore. His conduct as a soldier was exemplary ; he was brave, active and intelligent ; and while hostilities continued, the good opinion with which he had inspired his companions remained unshaken. At the conclusion of the war he returned to his native country, and for many years was no more heard of. At length, however, a letter came from him to Colonel Callender Irvine, son of the General, in which after expressing the most cordial attachment to his friend and benefactor, he added—" An affair of honour compelled me to abandon my own country. I fled to America for refuge, was graciously received by your venerated father, and cherished by him as a son. My obligation cannot be told—the powers of language cannot express all that I feel. I wish his portrait above all things—send it to me, that I may possess the delight of constantly viewing the resemblance of my best friend. It will fill up the measure of my happiness— I have content and opulence. The mistress of my early affection is now my wife, and mine is the honour to subscribe myself, the

"BARON DE ROSENDOLPHE."

OVUM REIPUBLICÆ.—*The Congress of* 1765.

[COMMUNICATED BY A DISTINGUISHED PATRIOT.]

SOUTH-CAROLINA is literally one of the Nine primitive Muses of American Liberty. "BEFORE THE THIRTEEN WERE, SHE IS." We must never forget that the parent of the Revolution, the very *Ovum Reipublicæ*, was the Congress which convened in New York, in 1765. But nine Colonies were represented, as four were overpowered by the Royal party. But South-Carolina beat down the strong opposition of the Crown, and was the *only one*, South of the Potomac, that sent a delegation. This was the achievement of General Gadsden.

In this primæval council, our members were far from being insignificant. Three committees only were appointed, and of two, the sons of Carolina were chairmen. Mr. Lynch, (father of the patriot who signed the Declaration of Independence,) was chairman of the one to prepare an address to the House of Commons; and John Rutledge, (who then was but twenty-six years of age,) of that for the House of Lords. This convention of sages, was the parent-plant of our present Confederacy of Republics. Thus was South-Carolina among the ab-original founders of the Union.

Delegates to the Congress of 1765.

Massachusetts 3.—James Otis, Oliver Partridge, Timothy Ruggles.

Rhode Island 2.—Metcalf Bowler, Henry Ward.

Connecticut 3.—Eliphalet Dyer, David Rowland, William Samuel Johnson.

New-York 5.—Robert R. Livingston, John Cruger, Philip Livingston, William Bayard, Leonard Lispenard.

New-Jersey 3.—Robert Ogden, Hendrick Fisher, Joseph Borden.

Pennsylvania 3.—John Dickinson, John Morton, George Bryan.

Delaware 3.—Jacob Kollock, Thomas M'Kean, Cæsar Rodney.

Maryland 3.—William Murdock, Edward Tilghman, Thomas Ringgold.

South-Carolina 3.—Thomas Lynch, Christopher Gadsden, John Rutledge.

Nine Colonies, and Twenty-eight Delegates.

Extracts from the official Journal of the Congress of 1765.

Met in New-York, on Monday, 7th October, 1765.—After having examined and admitted the certificates of appointment of the above Members, the said committees proceeded to choose a Chairman by ballot; and Timothy Ruggles, Esq., of Massachusetts, on sorting and counting the votes, appeared to have a majority, and thereupon was placed in the chair.

Resolved, nem. con., That Mr. John Cotton, be Clerk to this Congress during the continuance thereof.

Resolved, That the Committee of each Colony, shall have one voice only, in determining any questions that shall arise in the Congress.

After meeting regularly every day, with the exception of the Sabbath, they concurred in a declaration of the rights and grievances of America, and appointed the following committees, on Saturday, 19th October, 1765:—

Upon motion voted, that Robert R. Livingston of New-York, William Samuel Johnson, and William Murdock, Esq'rs. be a committee to prepare an Address to His Majesty, and lay the same before the Congress on Monday next.

Voted also, that John Rutledge of South-Carolina, Edward Tilghman, and Philip Livingston, Esq'rs. be a committee to prepare a Memorial and Petition to the Lords in Parliament, and lay the same before the Congress on Monday next.

Voted also, that Thomas Lynch of South-Carolina, James Otis, and Thomas M'Kean, Esq'rs. be a Committee to prepare a Petition to the House of Commons of Great Britain, and lay the same before the Congress on Monday next.

After having attended daily, the last meeting was held on Thursday, 24th October, 1765 :—

Voted unanimously, that the Clerk of this Congress sign the minutes of their proceedings, and deliver a *copy for the use of each Colony and Province.*

Having fulfilled the high duties with which they had been entrusted, they adjourned, and prepared for those scenes in which many of them acted with such elevation, and which have ended in the establishment of the happiest Nation, and noblest Republic on earth.*

---

* An authentic account of this Congress is preserved in the work entitled " *The Principles and Acts of the Revolution.*"

MISCELLANEOUS ANECDOTES.

JOE BETTYS.

At a convivial meeting, at which the healths of the captors of André were drunk, and a toast proposed to the memory of *Fulmer, Cory and Perkins*, who achieved the capture of Joseph Bettys, a distinguished traitor and spy, the venerable Colonel Ball, who presided, made the statement which follows:—

" During the war of the Revolution, I was an officer in the New-York line, in the Regiment commanded by Colonel Wynkoop. Being acquainted with Bettys, who was a citizen of Ballston, and knowing him to be bold, athletic and intelligent in an uncommon degree, I was desirous of obtaining his services for my country, and succeeded in enlisting him as a Sergeant: he was afterwards reduced to the ranks, on account of some insolence to an officer, who he said had abused him without a cause. Knowing his irritable and determined spirit, and unwilling to lose him, I procured him the rank of Sergeant, in the fleet commanded by General Arnold, (afterwards the distinguished traitor,) on Lake Champlain, in '76. Bettys was in that desperate fight, which took place in the latter part of the campaign, between the British and American fleets, on that lake, and being a skillful seaman, was of signal service during the battle He fought until every commissioned officer on board his vessel was killed or wounded, and then assumed command himself, and continued the fight with such reckless courage, that General Waterbury, who was second in command under Arnold, perceiving the vessel was likely to sink, was obliged to order Bettys and the remnant of his crew on board his own vessel, and having noticed his extraordinary bravery and conduct, he stationed him on the quarter-deck by his side, and

20

gave orders through him, until the vessel, becoming altogether
crippled, the crew mostly killed, himself wounded, and only
two officers left, the colours were struck to the enemy. General Waterbury afterwards told my father, that he never saw a
man behave with such deliberate desperation as Bettys, and
that the shrewdness of his management, showed that his conduct was not inferior to his courage. After the action, Bettys
went to Canada—turned traitor to his country—received an
Ensign's commission in the British army—became a spy—and
proved himself a most dangerous and subtle enemy. He was
at length arrested, tried, and condemned to be hung at West
Point. But the entreaties of his aged parents, and the solicitations of influential whigs, induced General Washington to pardon him on promise of amendment. But it was in vain. The
generosity of the act only added rancour to his hatred, and the
whigs of the section of the country, especially of Ballston, had
deep occasion to remember the traitor, and to regret the unfortunate lenity they had caused to be shown him. He recruited
soldiers for the King, in the very heart of the country. He
captured and carried off the most zealous and efficient patriots,
and subjected them to the greatest suffering, and those against
whom he bore particular malice lost their dwellings by fire or
lives by murder, and all this, while the British Commander
kept him in employ, as a faithful and most successful messen-
ger, and a cunning and intelligent spy. No fatigue wearied
his resolution—no distance was an obstacle to his purpose, and
no danger appalled his courage. No one felt secure. Sometimes in the darkness of the night he came by stealth upon us,
and sometimes, even in the middle of the day, he was prowling
about, as if unconscious of any danger. He boldly proclaimed
himself a desperado, that he carried his life in his hand—that
he was as careless of it as he should be of that of others, should
they undertake to catch him; that his liberty was guarded by
his life, and whoever should undertake to deprive him of it,
must expect to mingle their blood with his. And it was well
understood, that what Bettys said, Bettys meant, and, as well
ascertained, that when he came among us, to perpetrate his
mischief, that he generally brought with him a band of refugees,

and concealed them in the neighbourhood, to assist him in the accomplishment of his purposes. Still, there were many who resolved on his apprehension, be the danger what it might; and many ineffectual attempts were made for that purpose. But he eluded all their vigilance till sometime in the winter of '81–'82, when a suspicious stranger, was observed in the neighbourhood in snow shoes, and well armed. Cory and Perkins, on information from Fulmer, immediately armed themselves, and together with Fulmer, proceeded in pursuit. They traced him by a circuitous track, to the house of a tory; they consulted a moment, and then, by a sudden effort, bursting open the door, rushed upon him, and seized him, before he had an opportunity of effecting any resistance. He was at his meal, with his pistols lying on the table, and his rifle resting on his arm; he made an attempt to discharge the latter, but not having taken the precaution to undo the deer-skin cover that was over the lock, did not succeed. He was then pinioned so firmly, that to resist was useless, and to escape impossible. And the notorious Bettys, cheated of all his threats, and foiled in his most particular resolution, was obliged to yield himself a tame and quiet prisoner to the enterprize and daring of Fulmer, Cory, and Perkins. He asked leave to smoke, which being granted he took out his tobacco, and with it something else, which, when unobserved as he hoped, he threw into the fire, but Cory saw it and immediately snatched it out with a handful of coals. It was a small leaden box, about the eighth of an inch in thickness, and contained a paper in cypher, which they could not read, but it was afterwards discovered to be a dispatch to the British Commander at New-York, and also an order for thirty pounds sterling on the Mayor of New-York, should the despatch be safely delivered. Bettys begged leave to burn it, but was refused; he offered them an hundred guineas, if he might be allowed to do it, but they steadily refused. He then said, ' I am dead man ' but continued to intercede with them to allow him to escape. He made the most liberal offers, a part of which he had present means to make good, but they still refused to listen to him. He was then taken to Albany, tried, convicted, and executed as a spy and traitor to his country.

And, the only reward these daring men ever received for their hazardous achievement, was the rifle and pistols of Bettys. The conduct of the captors of André was noble, but that of the captors of Bettys was both noble and heroic. André was a gentleman, and without the means of defence. Bettys was fully armed, and known to be a desperado. The capture of the former was by accident—of the latter, by enterprize and design. That of the former was without danger; of the latter, at the imminent peril of life. André was a more important, but perhaps not a more dangerous man than Bettys. Both tempted their captors with all-seducing gold, and both were foiled. And, Paulding Williams, and Van Wart, though venerated in the highest degree by me, as having exhibited a trait of character, honourable to the reputation of their country, have not, in my estimation, claims to celebrity superior to those of Fulmer, Cory, and Perkins." The President having concluded, the toast was drunk, amidst the most thundering applause.

GENERAL STUART, FORMERLY OF WASHINGTON'S HORSE.

GENERAL SMITH, of Washington City, who visited Charleston in 1826, communicated the anecdote which follows to one of my most esteemed friends. I take great pleasure in recording it, because it not only does honour to the distinguished officer of whom he spoke, but affords a new and interesting proof of the enthusiastic feelings and attachment of the whig ladies of America to their country.

"General Stuart, of Maryland, who served at Entaw, as a Lieutenant, under Colonel Wm. Washington, and who in the action was severely wounded, being recently called upon to read the Declaration of Independence, before a numerous assemblage of citizens, celebrating the birth-day of our liberty, appeared in full military costume, fashioned according to the times in which he served. A friend familiarly commenting on the singularity of his appearance, and the improved style of modern military dress, drew from him the following observations:—'Our Regimentals, in former days, were fashioned according to the exigencies of the times, and were made more for use than show. I admire the ancient garb exceedingly, and but for the death of my venerated mother, should this day have appeared before the public, clad in the very waistcoat I had on, when shot through the body at Entaw. The good lady regarded it as a trophy, and earnestly requested, that at her death, I would allow her the privilege of carrying it with her to the tomb. I was sensible how much the affectionate feeling of parental love glowed in her bosom, and of the pride she felt that I had bled in my country's service. To have denied her request, would have evinced an insensibility, which I could never experience. Consent, on my part, was instantaneous and decided, and she actually wore the waistcoat in question beneath the shroud in which she was interred.'"

A brief Statement of the sanguinary mode in which the War was carried on between Whig and Tory while the British held possession of the Carolinas.

To give a just idea of the horrors which prevailed in the interior country, from the violence of party spirit, would be altogether beyond my ability.   Dr. Ramsay says,* " The destructions and depredations committed, by them, were so enormous, that should the whole be particularly related, they who live at a distance would scarcely believe what could be attested by hundreds of eye-witnesses."   It may truly be said to have been a war of extermination.   There was, however, one characteristic difference which does honour to the whigs. Unless in cases, where outrageous murders had been committed, or destruction of property wantonly indulged in, they were contented, when the power to injure was in their hands, to send the criminal aggressors within the limits of the British garrisons.   But insatiable vengeance uniformly directed the operations of the tories, and their triumphs were invariably sealed with blood.   Look at the appalling career of Fanning, Will Cunningham, and other British partizans, and contrast it with the mild and benevolent conduct of Marion, and of Pickens, and the truth and justice of my statement must be acknowledged, without contradiction.   Very many instances in point might be introduced in this place.   I have already noticed many in my first series of Anecdotes.+   I shall confine myself on the present occasion, in relating only a few, for the correctness of which many living witnesses can still bear testimony.   The toils and dangers of war had not steeled men's heart's against the influence of milder feelings, and the passion of love maintained its ascendency with its accustomed and resistless power.   The brave are ever the favourites of the fair,

* Vol. II. p. 34.   + Page 259.

and distinction in the field of honour, was found by the patriot soldier, the most certain passport to the affections of his mistress. Captain Tateman, a youth of gallantry, had successfully addressed a very amiable lady, and a day was appointed for the celebration of the nuptials. Repairing with his friend, Lieut. Geger, to the habitation of his mistress, he found the minister, the Rev. Mr. Thens, and company invited, already assembled to witness the ceremony, and believed his bliss secure. But the completion of his happiness was denied him. The news of the intended union had spread abroad, and the neighbouring tories having assembled in force, resolved by a decided manifestation of resentment, to mar the felicity of the parties forever. The house was speedily surrounded, and the bridegroom demanded for sacrifice. His presence was denied by the family, but no attention being paid to their assertions, sentinels prepared to destroy whosoever should come forth, were placed around, and the house set on fire in every quarter. Captain Tateman and his friend, who were concealed within, were warned of the fate which awaited them, by a sister of the bride, who had rushed through the flames, on pretence of saving some highly valued property. There was no time for deliberation, and the flames which were rapidly approaching, rendering delay impossible, they rushed forth, and running in opposite directions, passed the guard, and receiving their fire with little injury, found security in the adjoining woods. The Clergyman was dreadfully mangled, but on account of his advanced age, not immediately put to death; the remaining assemblage of male visitors, led to a distance from the ruins, and deliberately massacred. The torch of Hymen nevertheless, was not extinguished, and on the following day the nuptial benediction was pronounced on the enamoured pair, at a neighbouring farm. Such an act could not be suffered to pass with impunity. Vengeance was vowed against the barbarians, who had so wantonly outraged humanity, and amply taken. The tory party were from that day hunted down like wild beasts, and in a few months, not an individual among them remained in existence.

The unceasing severity exercised over the inhabitants gene
rally, and in very many instances by officers of high rank and
influence, gave birth to resentments so strong—to prejudices
so deeply rooted and unconquerable, that every serious evil
was considered as originating with them; every misfortune,
however trivial, dated from the period of their arrival in the
country. I remember, sometime after the conclusion of the
war, on a gentleman's complaining on a sultry summer's day,
that the wine before him was unpalatable, from its excessive
heat. A lady present, influenced by this universal habit of
complaining, replied—"Every thing, Sir, has altered for the
worse since the British came among us. We always drank
cool wine till then. Since their appearance, we have never enjoyed *that* luxury." "I was considered." said another, "a
skillful songstress, but the oppression which was meant to break
men's spirits effectually broke my voice, and I have never since
been able to turn a tune, or raise a note."

Themistocles being taxed with partiality in a cause brought
before him, frankly declared, "that he never wished to preside
in a Court, where he could not make a distinction between his
friends and his enemies." After the severe conflict between
whig and tory, in our interior country, to gain superiority, it
is not to be wondered at that the strongest antipathies marked
their conduct towards each other. An old Revolutionary Colonel, with whom I was well acquainted, presiding at a country Court, had a dispute referred to him, which had occurred
between two whigs. "I was never so puzzled before," he exclaimed, "to form an opinion on the justice of the case. Both
parties are staunch *whigs*, and honest men. Had the contest
been between a *whig* and a *tory*, I could not have hesitated to
decide; I should have concluded at once, that the former could
not have been in the wrong."

On another occasion, the presiding Judge directing the Jury
to give damages to a plaintiff, whose adversary had closely
attached himself to the British invaders—the Foreman addressing himself to his companions, said, "Gentlemen, a fair opportunity is offered us, of revenging the injuries heaped upon our
country by a band of traitors. Let us make this fellow pay

for the rest." Similar prejudices were as strongly felt in other parts of the Union, and, in all probability, deriving their origin from a similar source. A religious Elder from Jersey, making a voyage to Nova Scotia, became so completely dissatisfied with the soil and climate, as frequently to express his wonder, " for what use that country could have been created?" His pious principles, however, leading to the belief, that nothing was created in vain, led him to the conclusion, "that Nova Scotia was created, and especially designed by an overruling Providence, for the habitation of those pests of society, the tories and refugees of America, where, on ground, rocky as their hearts, they were destined to continue to the end of their lives, unacquainted with, and forever secluded from the privileges enjoyed by the sons and daughters of freedom." I have introduced these last anecdotes, merely to shew the mistaken policy of the British commanders in the moment of success, and the inveteracy of resentment that never could have existed, had victory been tempered with moderation and forbearance.

Nor were the prejudices entertained by the Royalists, less fixed and inveterate. There was a family remaining in the city, after its evacuation, which had once been kind and attentive to me, and to whom I ardently wished to be serviceable on every occasion. I had been successfully so more than once. Forgetting that the authority of the British had lost its influence within the limits of the State, an attempt was made, by getting possession of letters from individuals in Europe, to their friends in Carolina, to raise a tax on the inhabitants, which not being in the first instance resisted, became intolerable. . Notice was given to a particular friend of mine, that a lady in the city had possession of several letters addressed to him from England, which, upon paying a *certain postage*, should be immediately delivered to him. The sum demanded was too enormous not to be resisted, and my friend promptly refused to pay it, informing the lady that he should immediately set on foot an inquiry, to ascertain by what authority she demanded a postage for British letters in a city, from which that nation had but re-

21

cently been expelled. "Send me my letters instantaneously," he continued, "or my lawyer shall more particularly inquire by what authority they are withheld." The letters were sent, and after much entreaty on my part, my friend, who was well apprized of the hatred cherished by the lady against America, consented to let the imposition pass off without further notice. Gaiety was, at this period, the order of the day; there were no stiff ceremonious parties, but an universal disposition prevailed to be happy, and to dispense happiness all around. It happened that Mrs. Greene gave at the time a large and very elegant ball; accident carried me the next morning to the house of a non-admirer of the ball, to pay, as usual, a complimentary visit to the lady in question. I had scarcely taken my seat, when she said, "I understand from my *people* that a grand ball was given yesterday evening by Mrs. G. at head-quarters." "It was, indeed, a very splendid one," I replied; "exciting the admiration of every individual present." "Was there so much to admire," she calmly continued. "Doubtless," I replied, "as far as beauty could charm, and elegance of dress give increase to attraction, it would have been impossible not to have been pleased." "Your elegance in dress, I presume," rejoined the critic, "corresponded admirably with your taste in decoration." "It was, indeed, much the case," I replied—"the leaves of the Magnolia, hung up in festoons and decorated with paper shapes resembling the flowers, were so admirably imitated by Colonel Kosciusko, that many ladies forgetting that it was a season of the year, when few or no flowers were known to bloom declared themselves greatly refreshed by the softness and delicacy of their perfume." "But how did it happen," said the lady, "that taste was so much at variance with truth, and compliments paid, so contrary to every principle of propriety. God knows no head in that room was ever entitled to a wreath of laurel." I could only reply—"On this subject there necessarily exists diversity of opinion." It was for those whose views were disappointed by the termination of the contest, to cavil and complain; for those who had laboured for its accomplishment, to appreciate with gratitude, the blessings which it had bestowed on their country. It is not, therefore, to be wondered at, that their adherents should adopt prejudices equally strong, and think no terms too harsh, when applied to the supporters of the American cause. The term rebel, was familiar to the lips even of the most degraded beings in society. I well remember, that inquiring some time after the signing of the preliminary articles of peace, of a negro carpenter on my plantation, if a hinge could be found for a small gate I was about to erect, he replied, "I do not think, Massa, that a single British hinge can be found in our store-room, but I can make a rebel hinge in half an hour."

FRANCIS M'DONNEL.

SOMETIME subsequent to the publication of my first series of Anecdotes, in which I attributed to Lieut. Colonel Fleury, the honour of having struck the British flag, at Stoney Point, with his own hands.* I received from my friend Major Gibbon of Richmond, the following particulars relating to that transaction. "Francis M'Donnel, a son of Erin, emigrated to America previously to the Revolution, accompanying his father and entire family. When the American army was raised in 1775, Frank and two of his brothers, enlisted in the Pennsylvania line, as common soldiers. At the massacre of the Paoli, both of his brothers were bayonetted, which induced him to vow vengeance, and he accordingly continued with the army to the close of the war, distinguished as a faithful and useful soldier. Frank was one of the survivors of Major Gibbon's *Forlorn Hope*, at the storming of Stoney Point, and was the person who hauled down the British flag. This gallant act achieved, he was in search of his commanding officer to present his trophy, when he was met by Major Fleury, who took the flag into his own possession, but to Frank, who had been previously wounded in the breast, the honour of lowering it decidedly belonged. In reward for his services, Frank received a pension from the State of Pennsylvania, and subsequently, was pensioned also by the United States. He lived to a good old age,

* Vide page 211.

for many years in the service of Callender Irvine, Esq. Commissary General, the son of his worthy Colonel in the Revolution, General Wm. Irvine, but was unfortunately drowned in the Schuylkill, in the year 1820, near Philadelphia.

THE MISCHEANZA.

The dissipations of the British army, during the period that they held possession of Philadelphia, have been depicted in such strong language, as to stagger belief. If the representation is allowed to be correct, it can scarcely be imagined, that the Carthagenians at Capua, were more enervated by their sensualities, and unrestrained indulgence of their luxurious appetites than they were.

The celebration of the Mischeanza, appeared the climax of their folly and extravagance. It consisted of a variety of entertainments, got up as a parting compliment to the Commander-in-chief, General Sir Wm. Howe, whose want of success, had obscured the splendor of his early achievements, and who was now to be succeeded by a soldier of inferior ability, but exalted far above him, by the purity of his unblemished character. General Howe, by the influence of example, had broken down all the barriers of restraint; he countenanced every irregularity—neglected the discipline essential to the perfection of service, and rendered vice an object of emulation, as it appeared on all occasions the *first* and *surest* step to favour and promotion. General Clinton, was decidedly a better man, and probably, just as well calculated to carry on the Quixotic scheme of subjugating America, as any officer that could have been selected. I do not wish to enter into details. The pompous accounts that were given at the time, of the superior splendor of the various fetes—the gallant bearing of the *Knights*, displaying their prowess at the tournament; the beauty of the *Princesses*, lavishly bestowing their smiles of encouragement on their favourites; the brilliancy of the balls—the fascinations of the enlivening bands of music—the magnificence of dress, luxurious feeding, deep play and hard drinking, were well calculated to excite wonder; but in the eye of reason, cannot be viewed with too great severity.   I was told by a lady, of the highest respectability, at that period just entering into life, that she had herself expressed a strong desire to see the preparations that were making for the fete, and had solicited her mother's permission to indulge her curiosity, but that the sage matron gave a prompt and decided refusal, and turning to an old Scotch officer of artillery, who was quartered in her house, said " would you be surprised, Captain, if General Washington was to disturb the festivities of the day, and while mirth and revelry prevailed at one end of the city, that he should attack it in a vulnerable part in an opposite quarter?"   " Madam," replied the veteran, (who held the idle pageant in profound contempt, and had refused to witness its celebration,) " If Mr. Washington, possess the wisdom, and sound policy, which I have ever attributed to him, he will not, at such a time, meddle with us. The excesses of the present hour, are to *him* equivalent to a victory, and by us will be felt as a sore affliction to the end of the contest."

Something of the same kind was attempted in Carolina, but it failed in success.   The entertainment was called the *Cruadenade*, and intended as a fete to. celebrate the decisive victory *said to have been gained* by Lord Cornwallis at *Guildford*. It was attended by the officer's wives of the garrison, and some few of the sex, their devoted friends; but the ladies of Carolina kept far distant from it, with the exception of *one good whig*, who, at the expense of *feeling*, was resolved to indulge *curiosity*.   And she paid dearly for it.   A toast being given by a young lady from *Rhode Island*, of such sanguinary import, that I have heard her declare that her blood appeared to curdle in her veins, and it was with difficulty she could fly a scene where she was altogether out of her element, and where she ought never to have exposed herself to such gross and malignant insult.

MAJOR M'DONOUGH.

THE narrative which follows, relates to the father of Commodore M'Donough, the naval hero, so much distinguished by his valour and the victory gained on Lake Champlain over the British fleet, and I consider it altogether probable, that owing to his resolution, to relinquish his ardent desire for military fame, and to devote his entire attention to the education of his children, we owe the exemplary good conduct and triumph of the son. A day or two before the battle of Long Island, a Council of war, was summoned to meet in the city of New-York, which occasioned the command of the Delaware Regiment to devolve on Major M'Donough, the Colonel and Lieut. Col. being both members under orders to attend the Council. The Regiment was greatly distinguished in the action, and its Commander rewarded by the flattering approbation of General Washington. During the remainder of the campaign, it gained increase of reputation, but sustained some losses, and its Colonel being killed at Princeton, and the time of its service expired, it was disbanded. The zeal of Delaware was, however, unabated, and it appearing evident, that a new corps could, without difficulty, be organized, Governor M'Kinly assembled his Council at Wilmington, to appoint the officers, who were to hold the commissions, Major M'Donough, both from rank and high military reputation, was without hesitation named as Colonel. Information was immediately given that the honour was declined, and that his resolution to retire from service was not to be overcome. A gentleman of high rank was then appointed to command, but he, unwilling from a want of experience to occupy a post of such high responsibility, modestly said, " allow me to use my influence to induce Major M'Donough to take the command which has been offered to him, and I will willingly serve under his orders as his Lieutenant Colonel. His proposition was acceded to, and he immediately went forward, earnestly hoping that his mission would prove successful. Arriving in the evening at the Major's house, the purpose of his visit was made known. Overpowered by his feelings and due sense of the honour conferred upon him, he could make no reply; but having, after a time, recovered his composure, he said, "do me the honour of breakfasting with me to-morrow morning, and I will give you my answer." The visitor was punctual in his attendance, and was presented to Mrs. M'Donough, who set at her breakfast table, her children, all small and neatly dressed, being arranged on each side of her. She was an engaging and accomplished woman, who inspired with respect all who approached her; the Major, a handsome man, of very gentlemanly deportment. Breakfast being ended, and the lady and children retired, the Major addressed his visitor to this effect, " I am deeply indebted to the Governor and Council, and to you, Sir, for the honour of this visit, and the application which is the object of it, but circumstances forbid me to indulge my own inclination. The small farm which I inhabit is my only possession, and I am compelled, having some knowledge of physic, to make it a profession, the better to support my wife and the children, who have now left us. My heart is my country's, and I am not without ambition to acquire military fame; but, if I was to fall, what would become of them?" These few words, contained an appeal that was unanswerable. The Major remained at home.

Interesting Communication, relative to the family of

GENERAL LA FAYETTE.

During his late visit to America, he was approaching the town of Petersburgh, accompanied by Judge Peter Johnston, and B. W. Leigh, Esq. Addressing himself to these gentlemen, he said, " General Greene had made repeated applications to me, for certain supplies, which (the means being in my power) I was anxious to forward to him. But the frequent detachments sent out by the enemy, for the purpose of scouring the country, made the attempt extremely hazardous.

The British General Philips, was in possession of the town of Petersburgh, and had his head quarters in a situation very conspicuous from the opposite side of the river Appomattox, near which lay the army under my command. To gain my end, I resolved to make a movement, indicating an intention to attack his post, which compelled the General to call in all detachments, and out posts, the more effectually to resist me. I accordingly approached the river, and erected a battery, which I ordered to play incessantly on the house occupied by the British Commander, At the very period that my orders were executed, General Philips, who had been long sick, expired. I mention this as a remarkable circumstance, since, at a subsequent period, referring to historical documents, it appears that on the day on which the celebrated battle of Minden was fought, my father fell by a cannon shot, fired from a battery commanded by the very General Philips, who now expired, while opposing the son of the man, who had been destroyed by him."

The battle of Minden was fought on the first of August, 1759. In the French account of the action, which will be found in the London Magazine for September of that year, it is stated, " that Prince de Chemai, and M. de La Fayette, Colonels in the Grenadiers of France, were killed. The following extract is taken from the orders of Prince Ferdinand of Brunswick, issued on the 2d of August, 1759 : " His Highness is extremely obliged to the Count de Buckenbourg, for all the care and trouble he took in the management of the artillery, which was served with great effect ; likewise to the Commanding officers of the several Brigades of Artillery, viz : Colonel Brown, Colonel Huske, Major Haser, and the English Captains, Philips, Drummond and Foy." The order at large may be found in the London Magazine for August, 1759, as well as an article in these words : Head Quarters at Bielfielde, August 7th, 1759. His serene Highness, Duke Ferdinand, sent orders to Mr. Hedeman, his Treasurer, to pay the following officers of the British army, the undermentioned gratuities, as a testimony of his great satisfaction at their gallant behaviour in the late action, on the 1st of this month. To Captain Philips, one thousand crowns ; to Captain M'Bean, Captain Drummond, Captain Williams, and Captain Foy, five hundred crowns each. I hope the said gentlemen, will accept this present from his Royal Highness, as a mark of his particular esteem for them."

General La Fayette.

It gives me great pleasure to mention an act of disinterestedness which does him the highest honour. General Cotesworth Pinckney informed me, that when General La Fayette arrived, and paid his first visit to Congress, he presented a certificate, by which it appeared that our Agents in France had stipulated that he should, on joining the army, *be appointed Major General, and have a separate command.* This was decidedly objected to, and he was told that the Agents with whom he had treated had far exceeded their powers. That General Washington, in whom they placed implicit confidence, had been appointed Commander-in-chief, and that to appoint *him* to a command free from the control and authority of his superior was altogether impossible. "No man," said La Fayette, "can more approve your decision than I do. I ask no commission,—I solicit no command, till I have proved my devotion to the cause of America, and can come forward sanctioned by the recommendation of the Commander-in-chief." The battle of Brandywine speedily following, he obtained, by his good conduct, the applause of General Washington, and by his solicitation to Congress, the accomplishment of his wishes.

La Fayette and an old Soldier, at Montgomery.

When on his last visit to America, while at Montgomery, in the State of Alabama, he was visited by a veteran who had served under him in many battles, whom he immediately recognized, as an orderly and most gallant soldier. After much interesting and familiar conversation, the old man said, "there is one thing, General, which it puzzles me to account for—when we served together, I believed myself to be the youngest

22

man of the two. But my locks are now perfectly grey, and
you do not appear to have a grey hair in your head." "My
good friend," replied the General, "You are altogether in
error, the advantage is totally on your side. The hair of your
head is grey—while I cannot boast a single hair on my head—
I wear a wig!"

RED JACKET.

It happened during the Revolutionary war, that a treaty
was held with the Indians, at which La Fayette was present.
The object was to unite the various tribes in amity with America. The majority of the Chiefs, were friendly, but there
was much opposition made to it, more especially by a young
warrior, who declared that when an alliance was entered into
with America, he should consider the sun of his country as set
forever. In his travels through the Indian Country, when
lately in America, it happened at a large assemblage of Chiefs,
that La Fayette referred to the treaty in question, and turning
to Red Jacket, said, "pray tell me if you can, what has become of that daring youth, who so decidedly opposed all our
propositions for peace and amity? Does he still live—and
what is his condition?" "I, myself, am the man," replied Red
Jacket, "the decided enemy of the Americans, as long as the
hope of opposing them with success remained, but now their
true and faithful ally unto death."

*Opinion of General O'Hara, of the British Army, with re-
spect to the Soldiers of America.*

A GENTLEMAN of respectability, now residing in Charleston,
told me, that conversing with General O'Hara, sometime after
the battle of Guildford, relative to the comparative merits of
the contending armies. He frankly said, "as often as I have
been engaged in battle, I was never before so roughly treated.

Thrice during the engagement, I was compelled to yield, and as oftentimes was liberated by the gallant fellows I commanded. No battle was ever more obstinately contested. Both armies were entitled to entitled to exalted praise." I did not mention the circumstance in my first series of Anecdotes, but I perfectly remember that the gallant *Linton*, of Washingtons, told me, that in the action he had enjoyed the happiness of receiving General O'Hara's sword, who for some time remained his prisoner, though ultimately rescued by a superior force, which had rallied to save him.

GEN. CONWAY, a distinguished French officer, said to Dr. Rush, that he could drill an American in three weeks, and that the people of no other nation were so quickly transformed into Soldiers as those of the United States.

It was the decided opinion of General CHARLES LEE, that the peasantry of America afforded the best possible material for the composition of a perfect army.

And the *British officers* generally, not too anxious to admit a portion of merit to those by whom they were so often beaten, allowed, that though inferior in enterprize and active courage, the Americans possessed in a pre-eminent degree, what they styled *passive* courage. A firmness to submit to the frowns of fortune, and by patience to overcome them.

COLONEL ISAAC HAYNE.

Not satisfied with the notice I had taken in my first series of Anecdotes, of the death of Colonel Isaac Hayne, I had determined to enter more fully on the subject, in my present lucubrations, but the history of his captivity and death, has been so ably, faithfully, and satisfactorily detailed, in the first number of the *Southern Review*, by a writer completely master of the subject, that there is little wanting to give perfection to his narrative. I would only briefly state one circumstance, as it is a proof in point, that I have not erred in fixing the odium of this disgraceful severity on Lord Rawdon. "To render more effectual the prayers and petitions, urged in behalf of the unfortunate prisoner by his friends and relatives, the venerable Lieut. Governor Bull, whose character, loyalty and station, entitled him to the highest consideration, though labouring under a severe and agonizing disease, caused himself to be conveyed to Head Quarters, hoping to mitigate the sentence pronounced against Hayne. On his return to his home, the dejection of his countenance at once proclaimed the ill-success of his interference; it was scarcely necessary for him to reply to a friend anxious to know the result of his visit. "The unfortunate prisoner must die—I have used my best endeavours to save him, but *Lord Rawdon* is inexorable."*

* Vide First Series, page 250.

DUELLING.

I HAVE been accused by the North-American Review, of being a favourer of the pernicious practice of Duelling. I will state with candour the grounds on which this calumny rests. General Moultrie, after expressing great indignation at the proposal of his friend, Lord Charles G. Montague, that he should quit the American, and enter into the British service, says, " My Lord—I would make one proposal, but my situation as a prisoner, circumscribes me within certain bounds." And in a note, adds, "which was to advise him to come over to the Americans. This proposal I could not make when on parole." —*Moultrie's Revolution.*

The publication of this note has greatly mortified me. I had always believed, that nothing but the restriction imposed by his parole, had prevented General Moultrie from making an appeal to the sword to convince Lord Montague how keenly he felt the insult of his degrading offer.*

Upon this point, many of the friends in whose opinions I place the most implicit confidence, differ from me. They insist that from the previous intimacy existing between the parties, that Lord Montague could not have harboured a wish to insult the friend whom he loved, and that his sole aim to recommend the adoption of a line of conduct, which, without injury to his reputation, would infallibly prove beneficial to his fortunes. Yet Moultrie felt the offer of his correspondent derogatory to his honour, and rejected it with disdain. " You tell me, my Lord, that I may quit the service with honour and reputation to myself, by going with you to Jamaica. Good God, is it possible that such an idea should arise in the breast of a man of honour," &c. He felt as a soldier, and strongly expressed his indignation. How then could he, with a shadow of propriety, recommend to another a measure which he considered incon-

* Vide First Series Anecdotes, p. 16.

sistent with the dignity of his character, the honour of military profession, which at all risks should be preserved immaculate. I candidly own that I should have been better satisfied, had he said, "As a prisoner I submit to the insult, but were I freed from the restrictions of my parole, I should immediately call you to an account for thinking so ill of me as to imagine me capable of forsaking the standard I have sworn through every peril to defend. Feeling myself, at every instant, the insults and oppression of arbitrary power, witnessing the severities exercised against my friends and companions in arms, compelled to listen to the tales of sorrow of the widow and the fatherless, humbled to the dust and trampled upon, how is it possible for me to feel any other sentiment towards the men with whom you are associated, than that of determined and laudable animosity. The enemies of my country are my enemies; and as long as the hostile feet of British soldiers tread the soil of Carolina, you have only to look from me for every impediment to their success, that my duty as well as inclination would lead me to oppose."

I object with great decision, to the trifling causes of modern duelling. I have endeavoured, in several instances, and successfully, to calm irritation and reconcile the parties—but I must confess, that there are provocations which might induce a man to swerve from a duty which he ought to observe, a forbearance from which he should not depart, and at every risk seek satisfaction.

CELEBRATION OF THE BIRTH OF THE DAUPHIN OF FRANCE.

WHEN the soldiers of the Continental army, regaled with an extra quantity of spirits, (a feu de joie having been fired in honour of the birth of a Dauphin of France) had retired to their huts, and were in sociable conversation fighting their battles over again, General Greene, passing in the rear of one of them, was highly gratified to hear a veteran Marylander exclaim—"Credit is unquestionably due to the army before York-

Town, for their gallantry in compelling Lord Cornwallis to surrender; but while the shouts of our fellow-citizens proclaim their triumphs throughout the United States, I hope that it will never be forgotten that the army of Greene, took off the keen edge of the sword of the enemy, and made him a far easier conquest, than he otherwise would have been."

NOBLE-MINDED GERMAN.

In the Pennsylvania Packet, May 9th, 1780, I find the following Anecdote. The resolution of Congress of the 18th March, respecting continental money, did incalculable injury to many of the citizens of Philadelphia. A meeting of the persons concerned being called, a German, who had always proved himself a decided whig, made use of the following patriotic sentiments:—" I am now near seventy years of age, and have a large family of children to provide for; a great part of my property has been sold long since for continental money, which I have kept by me in full confidence that it would be redeemed at the value I received it; but I am disappointed, and am completely a ruined man. My losses are heavy in themselves, and my afflictions greatly increased by the triumphs and insolent conduct of my disaffected neighbours—yet I will never forsake the cause of my country and turn Tory. My fidelity once pledged, shall be sacred forever. The reverses of fortune may kill me—I may die of a broken heart, but I will still die a friend to my country."

In page 431, First Series of Revolutionary Anecdotes, a brief account is given of the expulsion of Congress from Philadelphia by a large body of mutineers, attached to the Pennsylvania line. The preliminary articles of peace had already been signed, and little prospect appeared of being again called into the field. The want of exertion is the bane of an army. Give soldiers active employment, and they only think of their duty; let them be idle, and they instantaneously meditate mischief. General Gates, says Dr. Rush, (Vol. i.) furnished me with a proof in point. Soon after his return from the command of a large body of regular troops and militia at Ticonderoga, desertions were frequent in his army while there was little to do, and yet during three weeks, in which an attack from General Burgoyne was hourly expected, there was not a man who quitted the standard of his country. But to come more to the point. The Pennsylvanians were clamorous for arrearages of pay, which it was impossible for Congress to discharge; and yet on former occasions, when destitute of food and clothing, and oppressed by disease, had conducted themselves with praiseworthy forbearance. I will give one instance of it. The badness of the roads had interposed insurmountable difficulties to the transportation of the provisions necessary for the support of the army. A scanty supply of Indian corn was the only esculent possessed. A committee of Field Officers waited on General Washington to represent the distresses and discontent of the troops. Dinner at Head-Quarters being nearly ready, the General, with his usual politeness, asked them to dine before they received a final opinion as to their mission. Various preparations of Indian corn, much of it parched, and nothing else, was served up. The committee influenced by the example of their entertainer, partook of the simple fare with cheerfulness, and never renewed the subject of their mission. The simple dinner placed before them, was a sufficient answer to their complaints, and their report of the occurrence on their return to the troops, silenced every murmur.

BATTLE ON PORT-ROYAL ISLAND.

WHILE I mentioned the gallantry of Moultrie and of the militia corps under his command, I certainly ought to have noticed the good conduct of a detachment of continental artillery, who, in no small degree, contributed to the success of the day. There were nine privates in the action, but several supernumery officers being at the time at Beaufort, who reprobated the idea of remaining behind in such a business, they marched out with the troops, volunteering their services as private men. Captain *De Treville*, commanded the gun carried into action;

Captain *Mitchell* pointed it against the enemy; Lieutenant *Moore* applied the match and fired it; Capt. *Dunham* used the sponge-staff for cleaning it out. There was one other captain present, whose name is lost, (probably Greyson, as he was an inhabitant of Beaufort.) Their gallantry met its reward: the gun was well served, and did great execution. And great credit was allowed to all concerned, for laying aside all pretensions to rank, when the cause of their country called for their services in an inferior station.

LIEUTENANT VLELAND.

Among the slain at the disastrous siege of Savannah, was Lieutenant Vleland. Born in Switzerland, he left, in early life, his native mountains to fight the battles of freedom; and entering a volunteer into the service of the United States, by his zeal and activity very speedily obtained distinction, and was commissioned in the First Regiment of South-Carolina Continentals. His enthusiastic ardour to obtain celebrity, attracting the admiration of a congenial spirit, he was, by Lieut. Col. John Laurens, entrusted with the command of the Forlorn Hope, which headed the Light Infantry led on by him to the attack of the British redoubts. In the conflict he fell, receiving a dreadful wound which rendered amputation essential, as affording the only chance of life. During the performance of the operation, (Lieut. Col. John Laurens and Lieutenant James Legare, to whom he was inexpressibly dear, assisting to cheer him by their presence) he once suffered a groan to escape him, when turning to the former he said, "Pardon, I beseech you, my dear Colonel, this weakness. My resolution was overcome by the severity of the agony I suffered. I will no more shrink from the trial ordained me." His fate was speedily determined. Spasms quickly succeeded the loss of his limb, and preserving a composure that could not be a second time subdued, he without a murmur expired.

23

COLONEL WASSON.

At the battle of Monmouth, Colonel Wasson, a distinguished
officer, attached to the Massachusetts Line, received a wound
which, literally speaking, stripped the flesh from his neck to
the extremity of the back-bone. Recovery was considered as
scarcely possible, but the Commander-in-chief, with whom he
was a distinguished favourite, that every chance might be given
him to effect it, had him removed to comfortable apartments
in the neighbourhood of the battle-ground, and sent a surgeon
of known humanity and great skill, to attend particularly to
him. Accident put into the hands of this gentleman, a quantity of Port Wine, which was essentially serviceable to his
patient; but the spirits of the Colonel failing him, and the sup-
puration from the wound becoming intolerably offensive, and
exhausting his strength entirely, death was considered as certain, and the opinion confirmed by a positive refusal on the
part of the wounded man to take either medicine or refreshment. This circumstance being communicated to General
Washington, who called to make inquiries, he said, with his
usual composure, "prepare your medicine, Doctor, I will endeavour by persuasion to make him more tractable." The request was no sooner complied with, than the General approaching the bed where Wasson lay, said with an endearing smile,
"Come, Wasson, my brave fellow, take this from my hand.
Believe me, you are too good a man and too intrepid a soldier
to be spared from our army. You must not die. We have
much need of your services, and you shall at a future day, find
your reward in the gratitude of your country." The medicine
was taken; and the Colonel, who was restored to health and
strength, has often declared that the encouragement given by
his beloved commander, operated like a charm, revived his
drooping spirits, and made the prospect of life once more acceptable to him. It gives me great pleasure to state, that Dr.
William Read, of whom I have so often made honourable
mention, was the surgeon who perfected the cure.

RIFLE-SHOOTING.

I REMEMBER to have heard General C. C. Pinckney say that he always found that expert riflemen made the best artillerists; and as an instance of the perfection to which they frequently attained, he said, " that observing one day, while the siege of Charleston was carrying on, a reconnoitering party of the British approaching rather nearer than usual the lines of defence, he said to Captain Mitchell of the Artillery, do you not think Captain, that by a well-directed shot you could damp the prying curiosity of those gentlemen, who are looking out to discover, if possible, the weakest points of our lines? ' Certainly,' said Mitchell; ' I will salute them with a shot aimed at the centre of the group, where I presume, the commander of the party has fixed himself.' A gun was immediately prepared, pointed by the Captain, and discharged. A great confusion was perceived among the enemy, and it afterwards appeared, that the shot which had been fired, had taken off the arm of Lord Caithness, who rode at the time at the side of, and the nearest officer to Sir Henry Clinton, the Commander-in-chief.

Correction of an error in the First Series, (page 97,) on the Authority of General Thomas Pinckney.

BOLMAN.

THE wish to free General La Fayette (said General Thomas Pinckney to me in a letter recently received,) did not originate with Bolman. He had distinguished himself by contriving and effectuating the escape from Paris, of the Count de Narbonne, a distinguished Emigré, whom he conducted safely to London. The Count de Cadegnan, Captain Bomville, and another gentleman, aids of General La Fayette, were stationed in London, where they formed a little council devoted to the object of liberating their General, for which purpose they were furnished by me with money, from the funds sent me by our government for the use of the General, being the pay and commutation while acting as a Major General in our service, which he had formerly refused to accept. These officers, to whom the escape of M. de Narbonne, and the means by which it was effected was known, engaged Bolman, to attempt the liberation of La Fayette, and furnished him with the funds necessary for the enterprize. Huger was not in London, but in Germany, where Bolman fell in with him, and made the proposal for his co-operation, which was accepted as described in the remainder of the anecdote.

LIEUT. COL. CAMPBELL, KILLED AT EUTAW.

An instance of his romantic gallantry occurred in service, which I will mention, although it may fix the imputation on me, however unjust, of being a decided friend to duelling. His son, who bore a Subaltern's commission in his Regiment, had quarreled with a brother officer, and some harsh expressions were eventually exchanged, when the dispute appeared to terminate. The indignant parent, insisting that a war of words was ill-suited to military characters, compelled him to call his adversary to the field, and accompanied him to it as his second.

MOB AT PHILADELPHIA IN 1779.

Early in October, in the year 1779, the peace of the city of Philadelphia was disturbed by a band of desperadoes, who, jealous of the prosperity and influence of many distinguished citizens, resolved on their destruction. When I name Mr. Wilson, Robert Morris, G. Clymer, all signers of the Declaration of Independence, and General Mifflin and Major Lenox, who had so often fought, that they might be free, I do not hesitate to say, that theirs was a blind infatuation—their guilt consummate, and beyond excuse. A number of the most enlightened whigs, to save the lives of such valuable men, determined to aid them in defending themselves, and repaired for that purpose to Mr. Wilson's, where the party threatened had shut themselves up. A mob of two hundred persons had assembled on the commons, composed, as it generally happens, of strangers and vagabonds. A North-Carolina Captain headed them, who immediately, with drums beating, marched his men to Mr. Wilson's house, and commenced firing, which was warmly returned by those within. No impression having been made by the fire-arms, the door of the house was assailed by large sledge hammers, and was yielding to the vigour of the strokes applied to it, when a party of the 1st Philadelphia troop of horse, *seven* only in number, and aided by two Dragoons of Bayler's Regiment, resolved to save or perish with their fellow-citizens. They were in a street contiguous, unseen by the mob. Dashing suddenly round the corner where Mr. Wilson's house was situated, the cry of "the horse—the horse" was raised, and their numbers not being known, the rioters fled with precipitation in every direction, but not before two other detachments of the same troop had appeared, who took many prisoners, and wounded not a few; the sword being very freely used, till opposition was no more. Colonel Thomas Morris, of our city, was one of the seven engaged in the conflict terminating so favourably to order and good government.

SECRET EXPEDITION.

In 1779, the Continental Soldiers, serving in South-Carolina, were unusually sickly, and rumours prevailing in the Northern army, that great mortality existed among them, Gen. Washington gave a special commission to Dr. Read to visit the State, and inquire into, and ascertain the truth, and return and report thereon. Arrived at Charleston, the Doctor had the satisfaction to find that the rumoured mortality had been greatly exaggerated, which, on his return to the North, being reported, there can be no doubt that the reinforcements ordered

to the South in 1780, marched forward with far greater alacrity
than they would otherwise have done. The battle of Stono
having occurred but a little before, Dr. Read visited the sick
and wounded on the neighbouring plantations, and on his return to Charleston, inspected the hospital, which he also found
in good condition under its medical superintendents. A visit
was then paid to General Moultrie, encamped with a considerable body of Continental troops and militia on the West end
of James' Island, watching the movements of Provost, who
occupied John's Island, on the opposite side of the Stono river.
Dr. Read, taking up his quarters for the night in the tent of a
friend, was awakened by a voice calling for volunteers on a secret expedition. Ambitious to engage in active service, he
arose, and providing himself with arms and accoutrements,
joined Captain Thomas Shubrick at the river side, who, with a
party were ready to embark. Moving forward with muffled
oars for some hours, the boat reached Mr. Robert Gibbes'
landing on John's Island, about the dawn of day. The object
of the expedition was then first made known. Two valuable
imported horses, Flumnah and Abdallah, were in the stables,
ready to be carried off by the British, who were about to retreat to Georgia. The centinel under whose care they were,
was perceived leaning on his musket, fast asleep, gradually approached and secured; the horses led out, mounted and rode
off to Stono ferry, where they crossed the river, and were
speedily lodged in a place of security. In the interim, Mr.
Gibbes raising up a window, said to Captain Shubrick, "Sir,
you know not your danger, a British officer of great activity is
quartered in the neighbourhood with a troop of dragoons—the
neighing of the horses when led from the stables, has, beyond
all doubt, given alarm, and immediate retreat is necessary for
the safety of your party." The hint was taken, and the party
scarcely embarked, when the bugle was heard and the approach
of dragoons perceived, but too late to do any injury. On returning to James' Island, Dr. Read immediately waited upon
General Moultrie, not without some expectation of being complimented on the readiness with which he had engaged in the
enterprize, but met with a stern rebuke. The whole transac-

tion was carried through without the General's knowledge or
concurrence. "I hate this predatory warfare," said the General—" give me fair fighting, when opportunity offers, and I am
ready for it, but this unbecoming mode, which requires more
cunning than courage, I thoroughly despise." No motive except the love of country actuated the soldiers of those days;
this long and fatiguing service was performed by Dr. R. altogether at his own expense.

ENLISTMENTS.

It certainly was one of the greatest errors in the American
system of warfare, aiming at successful hostility, to admit of
temporary enlistments, as it frequently happened that large
bodies of men demanded their discharges at the very moment
that their services were the most required. Some memorable
instances occur where exertion was paralyzed, and enterprises
the most promising relinquished, on account of this most unfortunate arrangement. I, myself, witnessed one of importance.
Colonel Lee had, with his accustomed sagacity, discovered that
the British army was vulnerable in a particular point, and had
communicated to General Greene, the probability of cutting
off the entire detachment of their army, stationed under the
command of Lieut. Colonel Craig, on John's Island. The plan
being approved, the troops detailed for the service were divided
into two parties, the one to be commanded by Lieut. Colonel
Laurens, the other by Lee, in person. Two evenings previously
to the contemplated expedition, I accompanied Colonel Laurens to the parade, where, in language as forcible as could be
used, pointing out the honours already acquired, and the fair
prospect of crowning them with additional laurels, he addressed
a Continental Battalion, whose time of service had expired,
and who were to commence their march homewards on the
following morning, entreating them to remain but three days
longer, assuring them that within that period, a blow would be
struck that would be heavily felt by the enemy, and cover

themselves with perpetual glory. But, his eloquence was of
little avail; it appeared that a pre-determination had been taken
not to listen to any proposition that would prolong their continuance with the army. One soldier, I well remember, exclaimed, " our zeal in the service cannot be denied; we have
strictly adhered to the performance of every duty required of
us, and our thinned ranks sufficiently proclaim, that in encoun-
tering danger, we have shown no backwardness, nor inclination
to shrink from battle. We were eight hundred strong when
we joined the army—we can now scarcely muster three hundred. Five hundred men have fallen by sickness and the sword
—it is time that repose should be ours. We retire with the
consciousness of having deserved well of our country. The
want of zeal to the cause can never be justly imputed to us."
Lieut. Colonel Laurens again and again endeavoured to rouse
the sense of honour, and to bring about a change of opinion,
but his efforts were abortive, and on the day following the detachment commenced their march towards Virginia. I was not
a little pleased by the distinction made by Lieut. Colonel Ternant, Deputy Inspector General, between such men as enlisted
for a limited period of service and those engaged for the war.
I attended him along the line of the company to which I belonged. On a soldier's name being called, he immediately
presented arms, and declared aloud the time for which he was
engaged to serve. Of such as were enlisted for limited peri-
ods, he took no manner of notice, but strictly to examine their
arms and accoutrements: but to every soldier who exclaimed
when called upon by name, "*for the war!*" he respectfully
bowed, and raising his hat, said, " you, Sir, are a gentleman I
perceive, I am happy to make an acquaintance with you."

CAPTAIN LITTELL, OF NEW JERSEY.

THAT many interesting Revolutionary anecdotes have been
lost, in consequence of the little pains heretofore taken to preserve them is unquestionably true. I have now an instance
before me, where a very imperfect account is communicated of

the gallant conduct of a partizan soldier, who, had justice been done to his achievements, must have appeared with distinguished eclat.

Captain Littell, of New-Jersey, was an officer of enterprize, and admirably fitted for the partizan warfare in which he was unremittingly engaged.   I need no better proof of his zeal and activity, than that Sir Henry Clinton, to get rid of the perpetual vexations which he caused him to experience, offered a considerable reward for his head.   His personal appearance was remarkably fine and imposing, from its strength well calculated to endure fatigue and privation, and from the corresponding temper of his mind, equal to the support of deeds of the most daring and hardy enterprize.   His influence over his neighbours was unbounded ; he could at all times command their exertions ; but not being attached to any particular corps, his services, though great, were passed over unnoticed, and while severely felt by the enemy, obtained for him but little credit at home.   In the winter of 1776 and '77, when the British had overrun New-Jersey, and established posts in most of the principal towns throughout the State, the successful enter-prize of General Washington in passing the Delaware, and surprising the detachments of their army at Trenton and Princeton, gave a new turn to the war, and compelling them to concentrate their forces, called into activity the guerilla warriors, who made it impossible for them to quit their posts without the certainty of great loss and not unfrequently of entire destruction.   On all these occasions, Captain Littell was pre-eminently distinguished.   On the day that Newark was abandoned by the British force which occupied it as a garrison marching to Elizabethtown, a company of Waldeckers was despatched on some particular service towards the Connecticut Farms—Littell and his followers speedily discovered and followed them.   Dividing his small force into two bodies, he placed one in ambush in the rear, and appearing in front with the other, demanded an immediate surrender.   The Germans wished to retrograde, but meeting with the party expressly concealed to impede their retreat, and briskly assailed in front, surrendered without firing a gun.   The British General, exas-

24

perated by their capture, ordered out a body of Hessians to revenge the affront; but the superior knowledge of the country
by Littell and his associates, enabling them to goad the enemy
at various points with spirited attacks, without any great degree of exposure, they were also driven into a swamp, and
compelled to surrender to inferior numbers. Mortified beyond
measure by this second discomfiture, a troop of horse were ordered out, but they in turn were routed, and only more fortunate than those who had preceded them, by being able, by the
rapid movement of their horses, to escape pursuit. A tory, to
whom a considerable reward was offered for the performance
of the service, now led three hundred men to the house of Captain Littell, who believing that he was securely pent up within, commenced a heavy discharge of musquetry upon it from
all sides. The Captain, however, was not to be so easily en-
trapped, and while they were making preparation to storm the
deserted dwelling, were attacked in the rear, being previously
joined by another body of volunteers, and driven with precipitation from the field. Littell, in the interim, with a part of his
force, had formed an ambuscade along a fence side, and perceiving the enemy slowly approaching, levelled and discharged
his piece, and the commander fell. The British, unable from
the darkness of the night, to make any calculation with regard
to the number of their opponents, were intimidated and sought
safety in flight.

My correspondent gives me reason to hope for additional information relative to this bold partizan, but so many delays
have occurred by the removal of papers on which he had to depend for information, that I fear, for the present at least, I
must take leave of Captain Littell. I think him an officer of
great promise, and it will give me great pleasure to bring
him more particularly into public view.

MRS. NELSON.

THE occurrence which I am about to relate, is given on the authority of a lady of the highest respectability—one, who I am confident, would rather perish than propagate what she considered a falsehood.

When Lord Cornwallis, on his march to the interior country after the fall of Charleston, established his quarters at Nelson's Ferry, Mrs. N. who was then a widow, received from him an assurance " that protection should be extended to her property, and that no injury would result from his stay under her roof." Mr. Nelson, when living, had manifested an unaccountable desire to possess a large quantity of plate, and had made considerable purchases of that article. On the approach of the British army, fearing the consequences of exposure, the whole was collected, and, as Mrs. N. hoped, buried in a sequestered spot, too well concealed to be suspected, and from which there was scarcely a possibility of its being removed but by her orders. Her calculations were altogether erroneous. Her secret was betrayed; the plate found, and triumphantly brought to view as a prize to the captors. Mrs. N. alarmed at the prospect of being deprived of a property so valuable, now thought fit to remonstrate, and in language the most respectful, reminded his Lordship of the protection which he had promised. " I certainly did engage," replied Cornwallis, " to secure to you the quiet possession of every thing *above ground*. What you chose to bury, I am not bound to protect. The prize must be given to those who discovered it." I do not entertain a thought that his Lordship benefited in the slightest degree, in the division of the spoil. I believe him incapable of such abject meanness; but by his countenance of the act, he sanctioned an unjustifiable theft; and certain it is, that Mrs. N. till her death, declared that the chest containing the property, was carried off in his Lordship's own private wagon.

WILLIAM CARSON.

AMONG the adherents to the British cause, there was not an individual whose inveterate prejudices were more constantly exercised to aggravate misfortune, and keep alive the spirit of resistance, than this man. Incessantly engaged in the attempt to excite jealousy and raise the indignation of the ruling authorities against the unfortunates within their power, his malignity would have been productive of incalculable mischief, had they not considering him weak and knowing him wicked, disdained to listen to his councils. I have, in the First Series of my Anecdotes, given an instance of his blundering propensities, in his address to *Provost*, partaking of a dinner given to him by the refugees from Carolina and Georgia, in consequence of his being the bearer of the grateful intelligence of the repulse of the French and Americans before Savannah, and the indignation excited in the bosoms of his companions in consequence of it.* I remember meeting with him in Edinburgh, in the year 1778, when being altogether ignorant of his real character, I accepted of an invitation to sup with him at his lodgings, where he assured me I should meet a party composed, as he stated, of friends to America. I soon perceived that it would have been difficult to have selected a company more discordant in political sentiments than that which I found assembled. Mr. Carson immediately made the rights of Britain the theme of conversation, and appeared to chuckle with delight, at the results that difference of sentiment, supported with zeal and strong indications of resentment, was likely to produce ; when Dr. Cooper, formerly President of the College of New-York, who was present, put an end to the altercation, by jocosely exclaiming, "We met, gentlemen, for convivial purposes, not to disgrace ourselves by indulging in inveterate animosity. In political creed, we are much at point and not likely to convert

* Vide p. 263.

each other. So fill every man a bumper, and I will offer a toast, which each individual may drink, in the sense that best suits his inclination.

"Here's *a full swing* to Congress."

---- ◆ ---- —

Ungenerous Conduct of General PIGOT, *towards certain American Officers, his Prisoners.*

THE same spirit of oppression that distinguished the conduct of the British officers in the South, was indulged and exercised in the Middle and Eastern States with unremitted severity. The news of the capture of Burgoyne having reached the American prisoners paroled on Long Island, Major Lenox, Major Hamilton, and Dr. Stewart, of the Pennsylvania Line, with heart-felt joy repaired to Flatbush, to celebrate an event so propitious to the cause of their country, so congenial with their own best hopes and most sanguine wishes. The night was passed at the festive board, but their conduct was in no way calculated to give offence. No symptom of exultation was shewn—boisterous mirth would have degraded a feeling of delight, silent but sincere. In the morning, a fish-cart filled with shad passing through the village, Major Lenox asked the proprietor "if he would sell a part of his load." "Not to a rebel-scoundrel," he replied, "though he were starving." This offensive answer was no sooner given than resented. Major Lenox struck the speaker to the earth. An affray was the immediate consequence; in which the American officers, as might have been expected, were overpowered and severely beaten. But this was not the last of their sufferings. Charged with an assault, and conducted before General Pigot, Major Lenox, in a plain, unvarnished representation of facts, related the provocation, and asked if it was possible to have withheld punishment from a rascal who so richly deserved it. "It is our business (said the General) to protect and cherish such of your countrymen as take protection. You must submit, therefore, to ask pardon for the outrage committed, or take the consequences that must inevitably follow." "Ask pardon of that scoundrel,

(said Lenox,) Never!"   "Will you, sir," said the General to
Major Hamilton : "May I perish if I do," was the reply.   The
question was put to Stewart, and answered with equal indignation.   "You must be introduced then,(said the irritated General) to the Provost Marshal: Mr. Cunningham, they are your
prisoners—you know your duty."   Six months of close and rig-
orous confinement, was the consequence of an act that a generous enemy would not only have thought just, but commendable.

GENERAL ISAAC HUGER.

In my First Series of Anecdotes,* I have given a striking
proof of the personal intrepidity of General Isaac Huger, endeavouring by example to inspire his men with courage, and
restore the order which had been lost in Gunby's Regiment.
I have a proof equally strong of his composure in action.   An
officer calling out to him, "General Huger, I plainly see one
of the enemy's riflemen taking deliberate aim to destroy you."
"That is no concern of mine," said the General.   "If you
think proper, order one of your men to take the fellow off."
"Dodge, or change your position," rejoined the officer, "or you
are a dead man."   "I will neither dodge nor quit my post,"
replied the General, "be the consequence what it may."

Fortunate Escape of Dr. WILLIAM READ, *and the other officers
of the General Hospital, from Massacre.   Furnished by
himself.*

GENERAL GREENE retired through North-Carolina with his
army and prisoners, after the victory of the Cowpens.   The retreat of the General Hospital from Salisbury to Virginia, being
in charge of Dr. Read, with a number of sick and wounded of
our army as well as of the British, it was necessary to proceed
with caution and circumspection, as the party were marched

* Vide p. 97.

through a country, some districts of which were decidedly in-
imical to us.   The prisoners frequently escaped, especially the
Queen's Rangers, who were seen in arms against us, in a few
hours afterwards, mounted, and joined by the country people,
watching every opportunity to impede our progress and capture
our men ; which, however, was generally prevented by our well-
appointed corps of invalids.   The young gentlemen of the department were in the habit, for pastime, to nickname our
party, and would play on the credulity of the country people
by calling one *Cornwallis*, another *Kniphausen*, &c.   Our
party had, indeed, a very equivocal appearance.   Many soldiers
wore scarlet, and some green, taken from the field of battle.
The jest was reprobated by Dr. Read and Dr. Gillet, a respectable Senior, who had joined the department, and our young
men and the soldiers were told that it was dangerous to put on
any thing like equivocal character in our situation.   Still the
joke continued, and went through the ranks.   Dr. Read sensible of the hardships and privations which the party suffered,
permitted this playfulness to go on for pastime, and did not
sternly put it down, when it nearly proved fatal in the following manner.   Halting one evening at the house of Mr. Spencer, the patients being a little in advance, the officers laid down
in their blankets in the hall of the log-hut to sleep, Spencer being at the time out with the militia ; the party believed themselves in friendly quarters, and dispersed with the usual precaution of placing out centinels.   It was Dr. Read's practice
to leave one of the gentlemen of the department in the rear to
remedy evils, stop hemorrhages, and bring in stragglers.   It
was Dr. Brownfield's turn that night ; when putting up at a
house in the rear, he heard a clattering of arms, and preparations and threats of an attack on the British party which were
at Spencer's : Dr. Brownfield got up, and convinced that it
must be our party, dissuaded the men, preparing to go forward, from proceeding, promising to accompany them in the
morning, and to be answerable for all consequences.   The Doctor saw at once that the *jest* had been the cause of the mistake.
An old man had secretly escaped from Spencer's, and given
the information, as Mrs. S. had (as she supposed) induced a

soldier to tell the truth, and she thought to serve the cause by destroying the British commander and his suite. The party came up in the morning, and we all rejoiced with each other on their providential escape. Their plan was to have fired between the logs, and then to have rushed in with swords and tomahawks to have finished the work of destruction.

-----·-----

PETER FRANCISCO.

Iꜰ it were an object with me to speak of feats of personal strength and prowess joined with consummate boldness and intrepidity, I should be at no loss for Anecdotes; for I scarcely ever met with a man in Virginia who had not some miraculous tale to tell of Peter Francisco. Romantic as his exploits were, and well calculated to afford amusement to the generality of readers, I shall mention one only, for which he was certainly entitled to great praise. A marauder, attached to a British Regiment of Dragoons, entered the chamber of a solitary habitation, where Francisco was sitting unarmed, and totally unconscious of the approach of an enemy. "Give up, instantaneously, all that you possess of value," said the soldier, "or prepare to die." "I have nothing to give up," said Francisco: "so use your pleasure." "Deliver instantly," rejoined the soldier, "those massive silver buckles which you wear in your shoes." "They were a present to me from a valued friend," said Francisco, "and it would grieve me to part with them. Give them into your hands I never will. You have the power, take them if you think fit." The Dragoon placed his sabre beneath his arm, the hilt of it being invitingly presented in his front, which being quickly perceived by Francisco, he seized it eagerly, and by a deadly blow, not only severed the head of his antagonist completely in two, but carried the division through the entire neck to the point in which they were united to the body.

The exploits of this extraordinary man have given exercise to the talents of the painter also. I have seen an engraving in which he is represented engaged in conflict with Five British

Dragoons, the whole of whom he made his prisoners; but I am not sufficiently acquainted with the particulars to give so gallant an action a place in these Anecdotes.

M'ELROTH.

THAT necessity has been justly deemed " the mother of invention," is strongly exemplified by the anecdote which follows: When the current of success, which had for a length of time favoured the British army, appeared decidedly to take a new course, and run in an opposite direction, Governor Rutledge, ever mindful of his duty, and anxiously solicitous for the welfare of his country, returned with all expedition to his native State, which he had been compelled to abandon, and evidently perceiving the advantages that would flow from it, determined to issue a proclamation, tendering forgiveness to all, who, from the mistaken idea of the inutility of resistance, or the hope of quitting the fatigues and dangers of the field, for the tranquil enjoyments of domestic ease and security, had submitted to the foe and sought their protection. So universal, however, had been the destruction of property, that neither types nor a printing-press could be obtained. A mechanic of distinguished talent, whose name was M'Elroth, was an inhabitant of the interior country; to him Governor Rutledge repaired, and pointing out the advantages that might be expected, from the wide dissemination of the contemplated proclamation, among the wavering and disaffected, earnestly requested him to prepare the types necessary for the accomplishment of his purpose. M'Elroth was a staunch and decided whig, but though willing to comply with the Governor's wishes, declared himself, from conviction, incompetent to the task. " I have never in my life," he said, " seen a type, or learned by what process they are prepared." " Your good will," replied the Governor, " will do much; your inventive talent still more, and remember how great the honour which awaits you, when it shall be said, that the expulsion of the enemy was in a great measure owing to your intelligent exertions." The experiment proved altogether

25

successful. Types were made of pewter, with a mixture of other metals. A press constructed, and the Proclamation of the Governor rapidly spread throughout the country—revived the hopes of the desponding—dispelled the fears of the timid —confirmed the steady adherence of the patriotic band, who had never shrunk from their duty, and roused the entire population of the State, to oppose the enemy with renovated zeal and energy, till their final expulsion and retreat from our shores.

SCOTT, OF JERSEY.

At the Battle of Springfield, in Jersey, a well directed shot from the British, mortally wounded Captain Thompson of the artillery, and a Sergeant of the name of Scott. The latter a North Briton by birth, inspired by an enthusiastic attachment to liberty, had, at the commencement of the war, crossed the Atlantic, expressly to fight under the banners of America. Colonel Forrest, who commanded the Artillery on that occasion, assured me, that on approaching the wounded men, he found the Captain perfectly resigned to his fate, while Scott was deafening all around him, by the loud tones and vehemence with which he uttered his prayers. Attributing his clamours to unbecoming pusillanimity, the Colonel indignantly exclaimed, " damn you, Scott, be less noisy, and if you must die—die like a man." The wounded soldier brought to his recollection by this reproach, immediately replied, " I will endeavour to do so, Colonel, and changing his manner, and the tones of his voice, thus addressed his companions: My fellow soldiers—men were never engaged in a more hallowed cause, than that which we are pledged to support.   If I, who am a stranger in your land, who came from a far distant country to fight your battles think so, and have sealed my opinions with my blood, how much more is it your duty, to cherish the sentiment, who have your wives—your children—your country, to call forth your unremitting energies, to expel the hostile invader?— Fight on then, with zeal and constancy to the last.   It is your comrade's last request."   When striving to raise a shout of encouragement, he fainted and expired.

LIEUT. REESE BOWEN.

At the battle of King's Mountain, Lieut. Reese Bowen, of Colonel Campbell's Regiment, raised in Washington County, Virginia, was observed while marching forward to attack the enemy's post, to make a hazardous and very unnecessary exposure of his person. One of his companions calling out, "why Bowen, do you not take to a tree—why rashly present yourself to the deliberate aim of riflemen, concealed behind every rock and bush before you? Death must inevitably follow if you persist." He indignantly replied, "take to a tree! no—never shall it be said, that I sought safety by hiding my person, or dodging from a Briton or tory, who opposed me in the field." As he concluded the sentence, a rifle-ball struck him in the breast. He fell and expired.

CAPTAIN ADAM WALLACE, OF VIRGINIA,

In justice to the memory of Captain Adam Wallace, I feel myself bound to give the following brief account of his bravery, as certified by a number of officers and soldiers of Buford's Regiment, at the disastrous battle of the Waxaws. Captain Wallace was posted on the right of the Regiment when the enemy made their attack, and was not a little shocked, after the exchange of a few shots, to hear Buford order his men to ground their arms. Captain W. so far obeyed as to cease firing, but speedily perceiving that no quarter was to be given, ordered his men to engage with their wonted bravery, and to sell their lives as dearly as possible. His personal activity and intrepidity were conspicuous, bravely defending himself against a host of foes : his aim was to reach Tarleton, and actually approached sufficiently near him to make several thrusts at him, though, unhappily, without effect. While thus engaged, a blow from a sabre on the back part of his neck, nearly severed his head from his body. He was found dead on the field of battle with a British officer slain by his hand at his feet. Colonel Tarleton, albeit unused to compliment an enemy, publicly said "the bravery of this man entitles him to immortal honour."

DIFFERENT MODES OF QUELLING A REBELLION.

During the mutiny of the Pennsylvania Line, Congress delegated one of their own body, Dr. Witherspoon, together with the Generals, Greene and Wayne, to endeavour to bring them back to reason, and a proper sense of their duty. "How shall we set about this business?" asked General Greene. "I would commence," said Dr. Witherspoon, by giving them a sermon. Religious admonition might be attended with powerful effect." "I," said Wayne, "would call for the aid of the militia, and such continentals as are faithful, and bring them to their senses at the point of the bayonet." "Let persuasion be tried in the first instance," said General Greene. Major Hamilton and another popular officer, were sent forward accordingly, for that purpose. Approaching the camp of the mutineers, a corporal stepped forward and exclaimed, "Major Hamilton, I wish you well, I would not harm you, but by the God of Heaven, if you advance a step, you are a dead man. This is no moment for negotiation." And the party retired. A much more effectual measure was pursued in Carolina, when the privates of the first Regiment rebelled, and set their officers at defiance. General Barnwell, an officer of consummate bravery, assured me that he could never sufficiently admire the calm and steady conduct of Major Pinckney, on so trying an occasion, for while other officers endeavoured without success to check the increasing spirit of insubordination, and with mortified pride found their commands resisted, and their harangues received with taunts and revilings, the firmness and decision of Major Pinckney at once put an end to sedition. Regardless of personal safety, he walked deliberately into the midst of the mutineers, and with a blow of his sabre, cut down their ringleader. The disaffected, who before breathed nothing but vengeance, without an exception, returned to their duty, sueing loudly for mercy and forgiveness.

BENJAMIN ELLIOTT.

OF this decided patriot, I have often wished to speak, because his devotion to the cause of his country was exemplary and unbounded; his ardour for military fame, pre-eminently conspicuous, and eagerness to engage in arduous enterprize so constant, that Pulaski, who had regarded his enthusiasm with a military eye, was wont to say of him, "here is a hero after my own heart. This is my own old soldier." I have but a single instance to adduce of his determined spirit, but that I think will sufficiently prove it. On the retreat of a part of the American forces across Ashley ferry, during Provost's invasion, the confusion in the rear was so great, that the boat was abandoned to the enemy, and even the tow-rope left uninjured. This was no sooner perceived by Mr. Benjamin Elliott, the gentlemen in question, from the high land, where, by a long causeway it was united to the river, than without consideration of personal danger, he galloped down to the river-edge under a very heavy fire from the enemy on the opposite shore, and cutting the rope with his sabre, allowed the boat, which was crowded with soldiers, to be hurried down by a rapid stream, the middle of which they had reached, and thereby removed from his companions all apprehension of further pursuit.

MRS. CALDWELL.

THE same spirit of deadly animosity which characterized the entire conduct of the British troops in the Southern States, marked also their unrestrained barbarity in other sections of the Union. There inveteracy perhaps was not as frequently shown, but where exercised, was in its consequences equally fatal. There were few occurrences during the war which excited so universal a sentiment of horror, or generated keener resentments towards the British, than the deliberate and sanguinary

murder of Mrs. Caldwell, on the expedition to Springfield. In
the month of June, 1780, during the absence of Sir Henry
Clinton to the southward, five thousand men and seventeen
pieces of Artillery, under the command of the Hessian General Kniphausen, left New-York, landed at Elizabethtown, and
advancing to the Connecticut farms, about five miles distant,
set fire to the village, and entirely destroyed the Presbyterian
Church, and fourteen dwellings and barns, leaving the inhabitants completely destitute, without food and without shelter.
In the neighbourhood lived the Rev. Mr. Caldwell, whose unremitted zeal and activity in the cause of his country, had rendered him particularly obnoxious to its oppressors, who had
even carried their resentments so far, as to set a price on his
head. Until this period he had eluded every attempt to injure
him, but unfortunately misled by too great confidence in their
generous use of power, and believing it impossible that resentment could be extended to a mother watching over the safety
of her children, he incautiously left his family at their mercy,
and joined the troops collecting to oppose them. The unpre-
pared militia being driven from the neighbourhood, a fair opportunity was offered for injuring Mr. Caldwell in the tenderest
point, nor was it neglected. A British Sergeant approached
the house, and putting his musket within the window of the
room, in which this excellent lady was sitting, surrounded by
her children, and holding an infant in her arms, discharged it,
and shot her dead on the spot. A Hessian Captain then ordered a hole to be dug, and the body thrown into it. At the
earnest request, however, of an officer of the New Levies, it
was afterwards suffered to be removed to a small house in the
neighbourhood. Mr. C's. mansion, with all that it contained
was then set fire to, and completely destroyed. Mr. Caldwell
was thus left, with nine small children, looking up to him for
support, without even a change of clothes or shelter under
which he could procure them refuge. But this unmanly and
cruel act did not escape severe and exemplary punishment. So
far from demonstrations of terror being exhibited over the
country, as had been expected, the inhabitants breathed only
sentiments of revenge. It animated the brave with new en-

ergy, and caused even the timid to perform feats of valourous daring unlooked for, and never before exhibited. The great object of the British expedition was completely defeated. The entire population of the country, thronged to the standard of liberty. The invading army was foiled at every point, and nothing but the precipitancy of their retreat saved them from entire destruction. It was on this occasion that Mr. Timothy Ford quitted his collegiate studies, and joining the army as a volunteer, received two severe wounds, which did not, however, prove mortal, leaving him at a future period to render those important services to his country, which must necessarily exalt his character, in the opinion of every genuine patriot, and every good and virtuous citizen.

PETER ROBESON.

PETER ROBESON, of Bladen County, was pre-eminently distinguished by his attachment to whig principles, and of course detested by the tories in his neighbourhood. Being on one occasion on duty at a distance from home, his house was assailed at noon-day by a party, expressly for the purpose of reducing it to ashes. Mrs. R. was ordered to remove a cradle in which an infant reposed, which not being done with the expedition required, one of the party overturned the cradle, to the great injury of the child, which, however, being speedily snatched up by the mother, escaped the flames in which the house was completely enveloped. Robeson, returning to the spot some days afterwards, gave indulgence to the spirit of resentment. Irritated by the loss of his property, and still more by the cruelty exercised towards his child, with a select party of friends, he set out with the resolution to pursue his enemies to extermination, and it is said actually put thirteen of them to death with his own hands.

GODFREY.

CAPTAIN GODFREY, and his brother John Dreher, were assailed by a party of tories, about thirty in number, headed by a British officer. Leaving their horses under a guard, these unwelcomed intruders quickly surrounded the house, when the officer entering with a few of his men, demanded of the terrified mother where her sons were. Aware that their object was to destroy them, she raised her voice, that they who were at the time in an upper room might hear and be apprized of their danger, demanding by what authority they sought them, and what they wished to say. The Captain perceiving a staircase leading to an upper story immediately advanced towards it. Her sons, who from the perilous position of their habitation, were ever in expectation of attack, and prepared for hostility, flew to their arms, and met their adversary at the head of the stairs, each presenting a cocked pistol. Lieut. Dreher, immediately fired, and mortally wounded his enemy, who falling back on his comrades, so completely intimidated them, that they fled with precipitation towards their horses, and communicating their panic, the whole ran off, leaving their entire spoils and property to the victors. The brothers, as they quitted the house, opened the upper windows, and firing several shots, gave alarm to the neighbouring whigs, who quickly collecting, secured the prize they had gained. Returning to the house, every attention was given to the wounded officer, but in vain ; he speedily expired, owning that his object was to destroy both the house and its inhabitants.

KNUCKLES.

IN the neighbourhood of Pacolet Springs, resided John Knuckles, an active enterprising whig. The whole of Union District witnessed his zeal, which caused him to be marked as an object for destruction, by those of the inhabitants who had given in their adhesion to the British commanders. Soon as a fit occasion offered for a display of their cherished resentment, his house was, in the dead of the night, surrounded, he was taken from the bed in which he reposed with his wife and an infant son, not a month old, and never after heard of. Some months after, however, a skeleton was found in the vicinity of his house, which was universally believed to be his.

TAKING THE OATH OF ALLEGIANCE.

WHILE the army lay at Valley Forge, in December, 1776, Major Forrest, having, in compliance with a general order, marched the officers of his regiment to General Knox's quarters, that they might take the oath prescribed by Congress, to defend and support the independence of the States, as declared on the preceding 4th of July. An Irish officer stepping forward, exclaimed, "before we go in, could you not, Major, contrive to see the General, and prevail on him to put little Ireland in the oath? "It would never do," said the Major, "but while we are engaged with England on one side, let Ireland sieze the golden opportunity and assail her on the other. Now is the time." "And so say I," rejoined the officer, "and if she fail to do it, let her sons from henceforth and forever boil their potatoes in a wooden skillet."

BARRY AND SWEENY.

IN my first series,* it will be seen that I had accompanied the British Commodores, Affleck and Sweeny, to visit Capt. Barry, on board the Alliance Frigate. The kindred spirit of brave men, caused them at once to discover each other's perfections. The intercourse of a few days, passed in friendly communication, made these sons of Neptune as intimate as brothers. To have seen them together, it might readily have been sup-

* Page 434.

posed that they had been engaged through life in the same service, and animated with similar hopes and similar desires, and had shared the toils and vicisitudes of war together. When the moment of separation arrived, Sweeny taking Barry affectionately by the hand, said, "Adieu my countryman!" "Not exactly so," said Barry. "you, Commodore, are a Briton, I am American." " I am," rejoined Sweeny, "an Irishman, and so are you, too, Barry, or if not you ought to be. You have too many of the strong features of a genuine Irishman for me to be mistaken in you. Your attachment to the cause of the country for which you have fought and bled, is both natural and highly to your honour, but by Jesus, you are too good a fellow for old Ireland to relinquish the claims that she has upon your best affections."

INDIAN ANECDOTE.

It is well known that the influence of the British over the various Indian tribes on the frontiers of the United States, had, during the whole of the Revolutionary war, caused that sanguinary race to indulge in every species of rapine and carnage. While in conversation with Judge Peter Johnson, at Abingdon, in the summer of 1826, a very plainly dressed countryman, somewhat advanced in years, passed by us, which occasioned my companion to observe " there, Major, goes a man, who has done the State much service, having by his active exertions cut off the last body of hostile Indians that ever committed depredations in Virginia. Murders without number had been perpetrated on the frontier, and many families carried into captivity. This man, with anxious solicitude, witnessed the enormities committed, and determined, if possible, to discover the path by which the settlements were invaded, the surrounding mountains being supposed to be inaccessible. Two gaps in the Cumberland mountain were explored, which appeared to him the passages selected by the invaders, as the best calculated to facilitate their entrance into the settlements. Information of the discovery was immediately communicated to the families the most exposed, with a request that on the very first appearance of an Indian, intelligence should be given to him, who had organized a party expressly for the purpose of preventing mischief. News soon after arrived that thirteen Indians, headed by a half-breed leader of great notoriety, had reached the settlement of a Mr. Livingston, and after murdering all the males of the family, were carrying off Mrs. L. as their captive. The heroic protector of the unfortunate immediately divided his men into two parties, sending off the one under the command of a brave and trusty friend to one of the gaps, and took post at the other himself, with the remainder of his force. Strict orders were given, on no pretext whatever to fire, but one of the men perceiving an Indian approach, could not withstand the temptation of making a good shot, discharged his piece, and with deadly effect. The Indian fell and expired. The alarm given, the invaders would have sought safety by flight, but a very heavy fire being poured in upon them, the half-breed and every individual of the party fell, save only one, who, terrified in the extreme, fled to the woods till opportunity occurred of re-crossing the mountain, when he gave so terrific an account of the slaughter of his companions, that the disposition to engage in enterprizes attended with such hazard of life subsided, and no Indian was ever again known to enter the settlements with hostile intentions. Mrs. L. on the report of the first gun fell to the ground, by which manœuvre her life was saved.

*A more particular explanation of a transaction recorded in
my first series of Anecdotes.*

IT is a fact well understood, that at the period of the struggle of party, in the year 1800, that General C. C. Pinckney,
by consenting to unite his name with that of Mr. Jefferson,
would have secured to himself the unanimous vote of the
electors of South-Carolina. But, consistent with his decided
principles, such an association could not be entered into. There
was no voting at that time for a Vice-President. By the Constitution, each State voted for two persons as President, one of
whom was not to be of the State voting; the highest on the
list, having a majority of the whole was to be President, the
next Vice-President. Now, if C. C. Pinckney had received
the votes of South-Carolina, which he might have done, had
he consented to a coalition with Mr. Jefferson, as proposed by
his friends in the State Legislature; these added to all the
Federal votes would have made him President. While he was
acting this noble and candid part, the Adams' party in New-
England were plotting to secure the Presidential Chair to their
own candidate, which they knew would be endangered, if both
the Federalists should receive an equal number of votes. They,
therefore, threw away several votes for the second candidate,
giving the whole to John Adams. It is evident, therefore, that
if General C. C. Pinckney, could have been guilty of a dereliction of principle, the want of faith to party might have been
excused from this instance of the conduct of the friends of Mr.
Adams. The opinion of the Ex-President Adams, writing to
General Gadsden, I have already recorded in my first series.
" I have been well-informed of the frank, candid and honourable conduct of General C. C. Pinckney, at your State election,
which was conformable to the whole tenour of his actions
through life, as far as they have come to my knowledge."

Imputation of Ingratitude incorrectly fixed on Republics.

Prejudices that are once entertained, are afterwards difficult to shake off. The stigma of ingratitude has been pronounced a characteristic of Republics—in my belief (as far as our nation is implicated in the charge) unjustly. I once cherished an opposite opinion. It was at a period when the inveteracy of party spirit assailed the fair fame of *Washington.* But I very frankly allow, that, even then, too hastily ; for by whom were the scandalous aspersions of character fabricated, but by a set of unprincipled vagabonds, the outcasts of their native country, and the scourge of that of their adoption. The gazettes, over which they had obtained a fatal influence, were filled with the most bitter invectives, nor did they scruple, unblushingly, to give the most upright and dignified statesmen of our country, the appellation of Traitor and Tyrant. Truth, however, in all its brilliancy, burst forth, and calumny was dumb. The name of Washington appeared without blemish. Specks in his character, if any such did ever exist, were no longer perceptible to mortal eyes, and by the universal consent of mankind, it is acknowledged, that as far as the frailty of human nature will admit, his character has reached the pinnacle of perfection. To the Hero, then, at once the boast and ornament of his country, to the immortal Washington, the charge of ingratitude is not applicable. Will not the liberal conduct of Congress towards the Baron Steuben,* Kosciusko, and General La Fayette, do

* When Baron Steuben's case was first mentioned in Congress, and reference made to the important services which he had rendered to the United States, the compliment was paid him, to inquire in what mode the sense of his good conduct could be most satisfactorily acknowledged. "By the grant of a specific sum in cash?" was his ready reply. This circumstance being communicated to General Washington, he, without hesitation, resolved to oppose the measure. "I am so well apprised," he said, "of the generous nature and liberal disposition of this excellent man, whose feelings are never so much hurt as when he witnesses distresses which he cannot relieve, that I am convinced his discretion would never be controlled by prudence, nor proportioned to his means, and that your bounty, speedily expended, would leave him more than ever the victim of poverty and distress. Essentially to serve the Baron, it is necessary to grant him an annuity, which he may use or abuse at pleasure. Inconsiderate expenditure may then subject him to temporary inconvenience and distress. But with every returning year, fresh supplies would remove difficulty, and his hospitality and kind-heartedness allow no diminution."

away the degrading imputation? Will not the expression of
the most exalted sense entertained of the services rendered to
their country, by the undeviating good conduct of *Jefferson* and
of *Adams*, prove the truth of my position? Will not the
eulogies pronounced throughout the Union on the good and
great, the *Patriots* and *Heroes* of the Revolution, confirm it?
Does not the celebration at New-Orleans, of the Victory of the
Eighth of January, give further evidence of it. And, finally,
will not the late proceedings in Congress, by which the pressure
of misery and absolute want is removed from the veteran's
habitation, and the bliss insured to him of passing the residue
of his life in peace and comfort, give ample testimony of a sensibility that is above praise. Is it not to be considered as a
noble and generous effort to do partial justice, where it is impracticable to give it full indulgence; and is it not an unquestionable truth, that the imputation of ingratitude towards men
who have served with honour and fidelity, is not attributable
to America.

LAUDABLE INSTANCE OF INDEPENDENT SPIRIT.

A FRIEND of mine (Judge Desaussure) travelling some little
time since in the interior country, lost his way, but was speedily put into the right road by an aged countryman, of tall athletic size, but very prepossessing appearance. He bore the
characteristic marks of an old soldier, and on my friend's saying, " I presume that you have served," promptly replied, " Yes,
sir. I was attached to the third Continental Regiment of
South-Carolina, and was twice wounded in the service;" shewing two deep scars, the one on his arm, the other on his head.
" I had an uncle in that regiment," said my friend, " who fell
when the attempt was made to storm the British lines at Savannah." The name being mentioned, he immediately replied,
" I knew him well, sir; and fought in the next company when
he was shot." " Do you enjoy a pension from your country,"
was now asked. " I do, sir, and have done so for the last two
years." " Why did you not apply sooner for it." " Because,"

he replied, raising up his tall form and stretching out his brawny arms, now, however, shrinking with age, "while these arms could support my family by their labour, I would not ask my country for help. After attaining my seventieth year, I found that I was growing feeble, made my application for assistance and succeeded, and now gratefully enjoy the bounty bestowed upon me."

LETTER FROM COOPER.

I HAVE noticed in my First Series of Anecdotes, my accidental meeting at Philadelphia with *Cooper*, of the First Troop of Legionary Cavalry, and the high degree of satisfaction that followed an interview with a soldier of such distinguished merit, after a separation of upwards of thirty years. I had then to mention his zeal in the cause of his country, his sagacity in gaining intelligence, his industry when in pursuit of honour, and intrepidity in action as often as brought into contact with the enemy. Such distinguished qualifications could not but excite my highest admiration and applause; but in a most interesting and affectionate letter just received from him, he has displayed a trait of character still more honourable to him, and more decidedly grateful to me. To give it in any other words than his own, would detract from its merits. He writes as follows:

"I had been separated, with Captain Armstrong and about fifteen Dragoons, from the rest of our Regiment, and had entered the British camp. In the interim, passing along the line of tents and seeing two horses with officers' portmanteaus fastened on them, he sent me back with orders to bring them off, but thinking, as I presume, that it had too much the appearance of plundering, he sent a dragoon to me to forbid their removal. Being now left to myself, and no enemy nearer than the Brick-House, where the battle was still raging, I deliberately rode along, inspecting their camp, when the thought struck me to set it on fire, believing that when the British saw it in a blaze, it would hasten their surrender, which I considered as inevitable. The wind was favourable to my purpose.

To complete what I thought of so much importance, I dismounted from my horse, seized a brand of fire, and entered a tent. The first object that met my eyes was a very sick soldier, pale and emaciated, laying on his straw, while at the side of his homely bed, sat an interesting looking female, the picture of despair. We exchanged looks, but spoke not. The tears chasing each other down her cheeks, were forcibly eloquent, and gave strong indication of the tumultuous feelings that agitated her heart. The appeal was sufficient. He must have been more than brute who could at such a moment have given increase to her afflictions. I threw the brand from me and rode off. To a sick soldier and a woman's tears, the British were indebted for the safety of their camp; and happy am I, that my intentions were frustrated, for their camp, without doubt, contained many sick and helpless beings incapable of shifting for themselves, who must have perished; whilst I feel conviction that cruelty will not swell the catalogue of crimes that may be registered against me."

GENERAL GREENE.

It is always grateful to me to relate whatever does honour to General Greene. "On the morning of the action at Eutaw, (says Cooper in his letter to me alluded to above) the firing between Lee's Infantry and a British party, brought General Greene to the front to inquire the cause. The General was so near me that our boots were actually in contact, when an aid-de-camp galloping up, exclaimed, 'General Greene, there is a large body of the enemy in your rear.' The General, without turning his head, promptly replied, 'Ride up to them, sir, and tell them that if they do not immediately surrender, I shall be under the necessity of cutting them to pieces with the horse.' The order was obeyed, and the enemy surrendered. I had been long accustomed to see men cool and collected in battle. But I shall never forget the calmness and appearance of unconcern with which the General gave that order.'"

PRISONERS CONFINED IN THE BRITISH PRISON-SHIPS.

It is a very happy trait in the human character, that proportioned to the pressure of adverse fortune, men's energies are frequently increased, and constancy sustained with a courage invincible. Conversing with my friend Chancellor Desaussure, on this subject he said to me, " I had ample proof of this when in confinement on board a British prison-ship. Every species of insult was offered to us, when we were marched down from the main-guard to the place of our confinement. We were hooted at, hissed, reviled, and ultimately pelted with every offensive kind of trash. Nor did we experience any diminution of injurious treatment, when fixed in our new quarters. Yet, not a symptom of despondency was visible in any countenance. A calm and dignified submission to an unavoidable evil, marked our entire conduct. To solicit attention from men who were strangers to the mild dictates of humanity, we well knew would be useless, and no appeal was ever made. When the more compassionate tenderness of the female heart led them to visit our dreary abodes, we received consolation from their attentions, and from the cheering expression of their looks, felt a revival of courage that fortified our hopes and bid defiance to the most envenomed shafts of tyranny and oppression. We were even sportive in our amusements, and by a variety of contrivances dispelled that *ennui*, which must otherwise have proved oppressively irksome, and caused our time to hang with great and insupportable weight upon our hands. We feasted luxuriously on the most simple food. Cheerfulness was our sauce and our stimulant to appetite. Our spirits were exalted without liquor. The cup of cherished hope passed from lip to lip, and the glow of becoming mirth and hilarity never knew abatement. In the consciousness of serving our country with

27

fidelity, we felt all the bliss of peace of mind, and if ever a sensation of sorrow was felt, it was when we heard of the dereliction of duty by some friend or person we wished to think well of; who, cajoled by the delusive promises of the enemy, or natural imbecility of their minds and temperament, had been induced to seek their protection. The establishment of an Ugly Club on board, was a source of perpetual amusement. For although there were some among us who did not quarrel with nature for giving us plain countenances, and who were not ignorant of their imperfections on the score of beauty; yet there were others who, without a single feature that could be deemed attractive, or a glance of intelligence or smile of fascination, lost their tempers, and were beyond measure fretful and peevish, especially when chosen to fill the high offices in the Society. But ill-humour was productive of no advantage to him who indulged it, and it was only necessary for a man to dispute the judgment and want of taste in his companions, and to attempt to stop the current of opinion, to have his claims to the perfection of ugliness fixed on him for life." The same happy disposition prevailed among the exiles to St. Augustine. Patience and equanimity were the order of the day, and innocent mirth occasioned the languor of confinement to be submitted to with scarcely a murmur, or expression of dissatisfaction. Two gentlemen, staunch whigs in principle, kept up a regular correspondence with each other; the one was an exile at St. Augustine, the other an inmate of the narrower limits of the Provost in Charleston. Some of the banished gentlemen, suspecting that the former was rather poetical in his prose—in other words, that he sometimes rather brightened the colouring of the information which he received from his city friend, resolved to put it to the test, and prevailed on Mr. Brown, the Commissary of Prisoners, who was about to deliver letters at roll-call, which had just arrived from Charleston, to place among them one directed to the suspected embellisher. It contained these words, " *Yahoo— Yahoo— Yahoo,——— ———* !" The letter was no sooner looked into, than bursting into an exclamation of rapturous delight, he who received it, kissed it with ardour, and handing it to his next neighbour, exclaimed--"read it, and rejoice, the day is our own; victory crowns our efforts, and freedom and independence are at hand." "I see nothing," said the gentleman who held the letter in his hand, "but an uncouth name thrice repeated, and followed by three scratches preceding a point of admiration." "The very cause of my joy," said the exulting patriot. You have seen the secret cypher agreed upon between my friend and myself, to communicate intelligence. *Yahoo*, stands for Cornwallis, and the three scratches gives positive assurance that he is taken." Strange to tell, this fanciful dream—this vague conjecture proved true. The very next vessel from Charleston brought intelligence, that propitious fortune, forsaking the standard of the victor of the South, that the renowned Lord Cornwallis, had surrendered his army to General Washington at York-town.

Brief Account of the Celebration of the Victory at New-Or-
leans, obtained over the invading army of Great Britain,
January 8th, 1815.

FROM the very nature of my work, and the terms in which I
have invariably expressed myself, the gratification must be
great to notice every occurrence which does honour to my
country.   It cannot, therefore, excite surprise, that the late
celebration of the Victory at New-Orleans, achieved on the 8th
of January, 1815, should be considered by me as particularly
worthy of attention.   General Jackson, the hero to whom it
was intended to do honour, has been regarded by me as a
bright luminary from the earliest period of his life.   I have
often dwelt with pride on the recollection of the manly firmness with which he refused to officiate in the degrading capacity in which the assumed superiority of an insolent British officer would have placed him.   I have greeted his first appearance on the field of battle, and his exemplary intrepidity when
there, as a fair and encouraging pledge of that perfect military
skill which caused him, on every subsequent recontre with the
enemy, to possess himself of the wreath of victory, and to claim
all the applause that a grateful nation could bestow.   The account which follows, is far better calculated to do him honour,
than any thing that can come from my pen.   It was furnished
me by an officer, high in his esteem, and possessing his most unlimited confidence—one who served under his command during
the greater part of the war, and who has often assured me, that
exalted as was his reputation for gallantry and military prowess, it gave not a higher claim to celebrity, than the talents and
virtues which distinguished his entire conduct in private life.
The particulars relative to the celebration, are copied from a
note on the subject, with which he furnished me.   He was
present during the celebration of this glorious national fete ;
and as a soldier and gentleman, I am confident that his statement may be deemed correct in every particular.

The late celebration of the Battle of the Eighth of January, at New-Orleans, is without a parallel in the history of our country. Those who witnessed La Fayette's reception at the same place, declare, that though extremely *splendid*, it was not near so *imposing*. Seventy-five thousand persons were present, while it will be recollected, that the permanent population of New-Orleans does not exceed forty-five thousand. What greatly added to the gaiety of the scene, and taste and splendour of the celebration, was, that the French understood more perfectly than any other people, how to arrange and give effect to these exhibitions. There were circumstances which took place on the occasion, that never before occurred in the world. A fleet of twenty-four steam-boats, almost all of the largest class, beautifully decorated, ascended the Father of Rivers, firing minute guns, crowded with citizens splendidly and tastefully dressed, and proceeded to a point three miles above the city; the place where, by arrangements previously made, Jackson came on board one of them, and from thence was conducted down the Mississippi to the battle-ground. On reaching the field of battle, addresses were delivered to Jackson in French and English, to which he made appropriate answers. The shouts of the people when he landed, greatly exceeded any thing which could have been supposed even in imagination. It was heard many miles off, and was the grandest and most sublime sound that ever struck my ears; for the effect of the human voice when combined to a great extent, operates on the mind in a most powerful manner. Among other things which rendered this wonderful celebration peculiarly interesting, was the circumstance that New-Orleans every year collects and concentrates citizens from every part of the world, and on this occasion, every nation in Europe was *actually* represented, and almost every State in the Union *officially* so. Several military corps also, were present from adjoining States. No party feeling dared to show itself; every man, woman and youth vied with each other in doing honour to the hero of two wars, the conqueror of Wellington's veterans, the guest of the State of Louisiana. The nations of the old world were taught a useful lesson, and could not *but allow* (in contradiction to

their cherished sentiments) that republics were *not always* deficient in gratitude to their benefactors.   During the week that
Jackson remained at New-Orleans, his conduct and deportment was most exemplary.   In Roman dignity, a *Washington*—in colloquial eloquence, a *Jefferson.*   His manners based
upon pure Revolutionary simplicity, every thing flowed from
the heart and went directly to it.

The speech which follows, gives in a few words the true
character of Jackson, better than any thing I have heretofore
seen in print, which I trust, will appear an ample apology for
giving it *publicity.*

While the company were assembled at the festive board, the
following toast having been given—

" *Colonel Arthur P. Hayne*—The compatriot of Jackson—
we tender him our hearty welcome to the land he so gallantly
defended,"

Colonel Hayne rose and spoke as follows :—

" Mr. President—Gratitude is not eloquent.   All I can say
on this joyful occasion is, I thank you—most cordially thank
you, for the flattering sentiment with which you have honoured
me.   Sir, if there be any portion of my life to which I recur
with peculiar delight, it is *that* period of it, when all the powers of my mind and body were honestly and faithfully devoted
to the safety and protection of this *gallant* city.   I can truly
say, that throughout that brilliant and arduous campaign, I
endeavoured to the best of my humble abilities, to discharge
my duty.   What a godlike spectacle was exhibited to the
world during the New-Orleans campaign !   It was there that
the brave yeomanry of the West, glowing with the holy flame
of Liberty and Patriotism, rose in their might, and conquered
the veteran troops of Wellington, and then was illustrated in
sober truth, the sentiment of the Poet, when he exclaimed—

> "On valour's side the odds of combat lie,
> The brave live glorious, or lamented die ;
> The wretch that trembles in the field of fame,
> Meets death, and worse than death—eternal shame."

" Fellow-Soldiers, you all well remember, on that trying occasion, that with one universal burst of patriotic ardour the cry every where was—*To Arms*—*To Arms*—your motto, ' *Victory or Death.*' The only contention among you was, who should be foremost in the race of glory, who most faithfully perform his duty to his country. And you can all bear witness to the truth of my assertion when I say, that in patriotic zeal and enthusiasm, in gallant bearing and daring courage, the City of New-Orleans covered herself with immortal glory.

"Mr. President—It cannot be wrong for old soldiers, assembled as we are around the festive board, after a separation of thirteen long years, to dwell upon the recollections of former times, even at the expense of saying something of our own actions. Bear with me then, while I feebly endeavour to place before you, one of the most happy illustrations of the moral sublime which was ever exhibited. You all remember, fellow-soldiers, when the Commander-in-chief was informed by the lamented Tatum, a veteran soldier of '76, that the enemy, in great force, had effected a landing. Then was it that the character of Andrew Jackson shone forth with surpassing brightness. Never, while I live, shall I forget his conduct in that perilous crisis, and truly can I say, that next to our God, we owe every thing to his skill and wisdom. When he was told that the enemy were at your door—had reached the margin of yonder noble river—I ask the question—emphatically ask it—was he not then surrounded by every difficulty that could possibly encompass the situation of a gallant soldier. Yet, gentlemen, did we not see him at that awful crisis, calm and self-collected—fortitude and magnanimity beaming in his countenance. *Yes, General, in your venerable person, by a delightful association of ideas, we were permitted by the God of the Quick and of the Dead, to behold once again on earth, our own immortal Washington.* And now the hour of battle is at hand, and we behold our Jackson placing himself at the head of only *two* thousand men, of whom not more than sixteen hundred were actually engaged, meeting a brave enemy, amounting in number to *five* thousand, and leading our eagles to victory and glory. The battle of the twenty-third of December, was the saving of this city. It was the great link in the chain of cause and effect, which produced the glories of the 'Eighth of January,' the day you now so nobly celebrate, brave citizens of Louisiana—a day, which records a mighty victory, in some respects, unparalleled in the history of the world. I must stop, fellow-soldiers, for the glories of New-Orleans are a theme too transporting for me.

" Mr President—I now beg leave to give a toast, and in so doing, to pay a small tribute of respect to departed worth—to brave and gallant friends, who bared their bosoms to the foe in the hour of trial and danger, and who, in the day of battle, were every where that duty and danger called.

" The memories of *Humphrey, Duncan, Read and Kemper*.

"Come expressive silence, muse their praise."

The Monody which follows, was written very shortly after the commencement of the war of the Revolution, by a young Irish student named DUNN, then attached to the Glasgow College. The name of the friend so pathetically lamented, was (to the best of my recollection) ROGERS, a native of Maryland, who, hastening homewards to assist in defending the liberties of his country, unhappily perished at sea.

PAULUS—A MONODY.

Upon a sea-girt rock Eugenius stood,
And viewed with steadfast eyes the rolling flood ;
And still, in every passing wave
He sought his Paulus' watery grave,
And fancy oft the corse descry'd,
Wound in its billowy shroud, and floating with the tide.

But far on wide Atlantic's dreary coast,
Beneath a promontory's shade,
The youth by pious hands is laid,
And vainly dost thou weep thy Paulus lost,
To distant shores and more inclement skies,
The faithless vessel yielded up her prize.

And are you then at rest,
The sport no longer of the watery waste,
An unprotected corse ?
The swain is blest,
Who snatch'd thee from the surge's force,
And hallow'd is the globe that holds thy clay,
And blest the pious youth that sung thy funeral lay.

28

But ah ! thy virtues could he tell,
Thy firm integrity above a price ;
Thy warm devotion to the public weal ;
Thy ardent friendship—honour nice.
Courage with pity still allied,
And modesty that like a veil did all thy virtues hide.

Could he thy innocence declare,
A grace so rare,
When linked with knowledge, that it shone
Complete in thee alone.
Could he thy love of liberal arts proclaim,
Still guided to the noblest end,
Thy country's freedom to defend.

Not to achieve an empty name.
For this thou oft hast conn'd th' historic page—
For this the jurist's knotty lore,
From Alfred's down to William's age,
Increasing still thy copious store,
A future gift for the Atlantic's shore.

Thine was the task her sacred rights to guard,
Her wide-spread States with friendly links to bind ;
The happiness of millions thy reward—
Thy monument in every patriot mind.

Soon as the tyrant spoke the word
Be slaves ! or dread the exterminating sword,
Britannia's hated isles you fled,
And mourn'd her ancient spirit dead ;
Your native woods you sought.
With Spartan virtue fraught ;
That virtue which can fate defy,
Prepared to nobly live or bravely die.

Behold the wish'd for shore,
The tempest howls and Paulus is no more.
Whilst many a mercenary host,
Securely glides along the hapless coast—
While safe the German transport bends its sails
And Caledonia's slaves arrive with prosperous gales—

Yet shall thy country's liberties survive—
Yet shall she triumph o'er her ruthless foe.
And Paulus yet shall live,
Whilst tyrants sink beneath th' avenging blow ;
Short is the gloomy Despot's sway,
But freedom's radiant form shall never know decay.

Immortal Youth farewell,—thy sorrowing friend
This last sad tribute to thy virtues pays,
Too true a mourner justly to commend,
And rich in reverence, though but poor in praise,
Yet shall Columbia oft thy worth rehearse,
When patriot virtue claims her poet's song,
Thy sorrowing friends repeat the solemn verse,
Thy native woods the solemn notes prolong.

DUNN.

CONCLUSION.

I AM not a stranger to the ironical compliment paid me by a good-natured friend, on the publication of my First Series of Revolutionary Anecdotes, to wit, "that I had given to the world, a pleasing and highly interesting *Jest Book*." This was, undoubtedly owing to the introduction of one or two epigrammatic effusions,* giving a faithful portrait of the talents and character of the British King, and the repartee of a witty lady to General Clinton, desiring the musicians at a ball to play, "*Britons Strike Home*." My intention always has been to give a faithful account of every circumstance relating to the war, and I freely confess, that I saw no impropriety, while I demonstrated how effectually we were checking the arrogance and foiling the intemperate proceedings of our enemies on one side of the Atlantic, to show how they were laughed at and ridiculed even at the fountain head of government on the other. A disposition to merriment is inherent in my nature, it was born with me, and I trust, that while life remains, I shall never be abandoned by it. My favourite maxim is,

"With mirth and laughter let old wrinkles come."

While, therefore, I plead guilty to the charge, and confess my crime, I trust I may still be allowed, from the Gazettes of our foe to show how idle and farcical the attempts to subjugate America were considered in England, and with what keen and pointed satire the administration were assailed, even at the seat of government. I will, in mercy, however, add two short pieces *only*, lest I cause the bile of my friend to overflow, and occasion him

"To creep into a jaundice by being peevish."

---

* Vide pp. 412-13.

The Cerberus Frigate being selected at the commencement of the Revolutionary war, to convey to Boston the British Generals appointed to command, the following epigram appeared in a morning paper :—

> " Behold the Cerberus the Atlantic plough,
> Her precious cargo—Burgoyne, Clinton, How.
> Bow, wow, wow."

HEADS.

Tune—*"Derry Down."*

Ye wrong heads, and strong heads, attend to my strains,
Ye dear heads, and queer heads, and heads without brains ;
Ye thick skulls and quick skulls, and heads great and small,
And ye heads that aspire to be heads over all.
Enough might be said, durst I venture my rhymes,
Of crowned heads, and round heads, of these modern times ;
This slippery path let me cautiously tread,
The Neck else will answer, perhaps for the Head.
The Heads of the Church, and the Heads of the State,
Have taught much, and wrote much, too much to repeat ;
On the neck of corruption, uplifted 'tis said,
Some rulers, alas, are too high by the head.
Ye schemers and dreamers of politic things,
Projecting the downfall of Kingdoms and Kings,
Can your wisdom declare, how the body is fed,
When the members rebel, and wage war with the head.
On Britannia's bosom sweet Liberty smiled.
The parent grew strong while she fostered the child :
Ill-treating her offspring, a fever she bred,
Which contracted her limbs and distracted her head.
Ye learned State Doctors, your labours are vain,
Proceeding by bleeding to settle her brain ;
Much less can your art the *lost members* restore,
Amputation must follow—perhaps, *something* more.
Pale Goddess of whim, when with cheeks lean or full,
Thy influence seizes an Englishman's skull ;
He blunders, yet wonders his schemes ever fail,
Though often mistaking the head for the tail.

Derry Down.

INDEX TO VOLUME THIRD.

www.ingramcontent.com/pod-product-compliance
Lightning Source LLC
Chambersburg PA
CBHW020104030726
47498CB00006B/1944